To Don Jeen , (F.H.!.)
With best wishes for
1976.

Martin Jarman.
December 1975.

THE HEINEMANN

ACCOUNTANCY AND ADMINISTRATION SERIES

General Editor:

J. BATTY, D.Com.(S.A.), M.Com.(Dunelm), A.C.M.A.,
M.Inst.A.M., M.B.I.M.

FACTORING AND FINANCE

FACTORING AND FINANCE

MARTIN FORMAN, B.Sc. (Econ.)

and

JOHN GILBERT, A.C.A.

HEINEMANN : LONDON

William Heinemann Ltd

15 Queen St, Mayfair, London W1X 8BE

LONDON   MELBOURNE   TORONTO
JOHANNESBURG   AUCKLAND

Printed in Great Britain by
Cox & Wyman Ltd, Fakenham

Editor's Foreword

The Heinemann Accountancy and Administration Series is intended to fill a gap in the literature that caters for accountants, company secretaries, and similar professional people who are engaged in giving a vital information service to management. Due recognition is given to the fact that there are two distinct bodies of readers: those who aspire to professional status—the students—and others who are already managing or servicing management. Whenever possible the books are written with this distinction in mind.

The management of finance is of vital importance to any business, especially when it is attempting to grow. Careful planning and control of cash resources is imperative.

This is a world of specialization! With the complexities of international trade and the varying requirements in different countries, as well as possible domestic problems, it becomes imperative to know the possible cash flow. Factoring, in its modern form, can offer a wide range of related services which can assist in this vital function of maximizing cash utilization.

The authors both hold senior positions within a factoring company. Accordingly, they write with experience and conviction. They have presented a comprehensive and unbiased coverage of factoring in a modern economy. It is a pleasure to include this book in the series.

J. BATTY

Preface

When factoring was introduced into the United Kingdom in the early 1960s it was almost entirely unknown as a management and financial tool. This was so in every industrialized country except the United States, the home of modern factoring. Even in America factoring was, and still is, concentrated heavily in the textile and associated industries and outside these areas many businessmen and financial advisors were, and are, ignorant of the exact role of the modern factor. In the United Kingdom factoring had become an accepted technique by the mid 1970s, by which time factored sales were running at an annual rate in excess of £300 million with considerable scope for expansion. All the major clearing banks, among others, had factoring companies or divisions through which factoring facilities could be offered to their wide range of industrial and commercial clients.

The increasing involvement of banks in factoring, in the United Kingdom and America, and indeed throughout the industrialized world, has helped to put factoring on the industrial and commercial map; and yet we have found that the marketing of factoring from inside as well as outside the banking sector, or by companies in which a major bank has a substantial interest, has exacerbated the very misconceptions that a wider acceptance of factoring should dispel. In particular, the association of factoring with banking leads it to be viewed solely, and incorrectly, from a financial viewpoint and as an alternative 'banking facility' managed according to banking criteria. In consequence there is a disproportionate lack of emphasis upon the administrative and credit control services offered by the factor and his attitude towards facilities utilized by clients. We believe this imbalance should be corrected and that a realistic and reasoned appraisal of the administrative services offered by the factor, and his proper place in the financial plan of the individual company, should be available to the business and financial community. It is for this reason that we have written this book and decided upon its scope and emphasis.

At present there are very few books on factoring available to the public written by executives operating within the industry. While many articles have been written in the financial and commercial press, we do not believe these are adequate for those who may wish to use a factor, or may be in need of a factor without realizing this fact, or for those who are called upon to advise a prospective factoring client. This book should be of use to those responsible for the financial and credit control plans of their company: the managing director or chairman of the smaller company, or financial director, chief accountant, or credit controller of the larger company. Of even more importance, we hope it is sufficiently detailed to enable accountants and other financial advisors, lawyers, credit insurance brokers, and bankers not directly concerned in the factoring process, to give a comprehensive picture of the service that can be expected, the resulting costs and obligations, the selection of a factor, and how factoring fits into the financial and administrative plans of a company. Finally, while factoring is rarely found today in the syllabus of economics or business courses, we would expect penetration to increase in this area with the expansion of factoring. Therefore the student undertaking such courses may find the ideas and information in this book of some value.

In planning this book we have attempted to set factoring within its proper financial perspective. First we give a brief introduction to factoring and various commonly used terms. We have then devoted the first part to the need for finance and financial planning, and the relevance of factoring, together with an outline of its development, scope, and general administrative and financial effect, both at national level and at that of the individual company. The second part focuses upon the management of working capital, the area upon which factoring has a direct financial impact. Finally, the third part investigates factoring in detail, as applied to domestic and international transactions. A word of caution is advisable at this stage. We have attempted to present factoring within a world context, particularly bearing in mind its American origins. The principles and practices detailed are, we believe, applicable generally. However, details of operations and legal status may vary between countries, if only to conform with different codes of law or business practices.

Information for this book has been gathered from many sources. It is appropriate to record our appreciation to our Associates throughout the Walter E. Heller International Corporation Network for providing detailed information covering local conditions. A special recognition is due to Mr. S. A. Lewy of the Walter E. Heller Overseas Corporation office in Chicago, to whom we are indebted for information and material relating to factoring in America, the country in which it evolved into its modern form.

Finally, thanks are due to our long-suffering secretaries, particularly Miss A. Curr, Miss J. Tennant, and Mrs. J. Harris, for typing the original manuscript and enduring, together with our wives, Linda and Priscilla, the elations and depressions of the budding author.

MARTIN FORMAN
JOHN GILBERT

Contents

1 Factoring: An Introduction

This introduction is designed to enable the reader to place various terms that will be used throughout this book into their correct context. In discussing the relationship between factoring and finance we are assuming an immediate familiarity with the nature and practice of factoring which should be established here.

1.1 THE NATURE AND PRACTICE OF FACTORING

The factoring process involves the selling of trade debts on a continuing basis by the client, the supplier, to his factor. The customer of the supplier becomes a debtor of the factor and has to pay the factor directly in order to discharge the debt. The factor will maintain all necessary records in order to collect debts purchased and will carry out all procedures that are appropriate for collection. The distinguishing characteristic of factoring as practised generally in the U.S.A. and the United Kingdom, as well as in some other countries, is that if the customer is unable to pay then the factor will bear the loss if he has previously approved the credit upon and the sale to that customer.

Having purchased debts from the client, the factor will pay for those debts either substantially at the time of purchase, or upon collection, or on a maturity date which will be fixed in relation to the maturity date of the invoices purchased. In any event the factor will be a debtor to the client, owing either the whole or part of the debt until the final payment. The financial effect on the client is equivalent either to selling all debts on approximately seven-day terms instead of normal credit terms, or to receiving all moneys for debts on a certain date from one debtor without credit risk.

The factor must carry out the following functions in order to operate a facility for the benefit of both client and factor. These functions replace those previously carried out by the client.

1. *Credit Investigation and Protection*

In order to approve a credit sale to a customer the factor must investigate how much credit should be extended to that customer. Information must be obtained from public records and other sources, both inside and outside the offices of the factor. Systematic collation and evaluation of such information must be undertaken.

2. Sales Ledger Accounting

The factor must maintain an account for each customer of all items owing to him, so that collection can occur when appropriate. The factor will also maintain a record of his indebtedness to his client, consisting of the difference between the value of debts purchased and moneys paid on account of such debts.

3. Collection of Debts

When individual debts become due from the customer, the factor will undertake all collection activity that is necessary.

For these services the factor charges a fee to the client which normally falls between $\frac{3}{4}$ per cent and 2 per cent of debts purchased. If the factor is making payments for such debts prior to maturity, then he charges the client at a rate usually equivalent to that charged by a bank for moneys extended to the client.

1.2　TERMS AND DEFINITIONS

Definitions of terms used in this book are as follows.

Client

The supplier of goods or services with whom the factor has a factoring agreement.

Customer

The recipient of goods or services from the client, who becomes the debtor of the factor as a consequence of the purchase of the trade debt arising from the rendering of such goods or services.

With recourse (or client risk) trade debt

A debt which is purchased by the factor from the client on the basis that if the customer is financially unable to pay then the client must pay the factor in respect of such debt. A contingent liability remains with the client for such debts.

Without recourse (or factors risk) trade debt

A debt which is purchased by the factor from the client on the basis that if the customer is financially unable to pay then the factor must take such loss. A contingent liability does not exist for the client.

Note: Both 'With recourse' and 'Without recourse' are used in other phrases such as 'without recourse factoring facility'. The latter term means a facility where as a general rule the factor does not have recourse to the client in the event of the customer's inability to pay.

Maturity date

A date agreed between the factor and the client as to when any debt should be paid in practice by the customer to the factor. This date is usually arrived at by a review of actual experience and can be related to an agreed number of days past due date of each invoice, or calculated according to an average expected credit period.

'Old line' or 'full' factoring

A factoring facility involving purchase of trade debts by the factor from the client without recourse to the client, and with payment of up to an agreed percentage of trade debts purchased being made by the factor prior to the agreed maturity or collection date.

'Maturity' factoring

A factoring facility involving purchase of trade debts by the factor from the client without recourse to the client, and with payment by the factor for trade debts purchased being made at an agreed maturity date.

1.3 COMMON MISCONCEPTIONS

Misconceptions abound regarding factoring. Even at this stage it is worth disposing of some of the more prevalent and erroneous opinions.

1. *Factoring is purely a financial arrangement.* This view is incorrect because the very nature of factoring presupposes the ability of the factor to investigate customer creditworthiness and grant credit protection. In addition the client is relieved of sales ledger administration and collection activity. The financial arrangement and its effect will depend upon the type of factoring facility enjoyed by the client.

2. *Factoring is an expensive financial arrangement.* This misconception is built upon the first, and is based on calculation of the total costs, including

the administrative charge, and relating these to any payments made by the factor for trade debts purchased prior to maturity. Any true calculation must take into account savings both tangible and intangible that are enjoyed by the client to arrive at a net cost which should be compared with the resulting benefits.

3. *Factoring is a short-term arrangement which a company will dispense with as soon as possible.* This proposition confuses factoring with invoice discounting or accounts receivable financing. It also fails to relate the financial benefits of those facilities to their cost. Many factoring clients will continue with their factor when they have no need for financial assistance at all. In fact the portfolio of many long-established factoring houses will show that many clients have been factoring for periods well in excess of ten years. The various advantages of the factoring facility can apply at different stages of the life cycle of any individual firm.

Part One: The Relationship between Factoring and Finance

2 The Need for Finance and a Financial Policy

2.1 THE FINANCE FUNCTION

The life cycle of a firm is often depicted as an S-shaped curve as shown in Figure 2.1. The figure represents the hypothetical life cycle of a firm, and

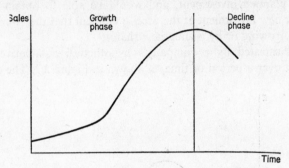

FIGURE 2.1. Hypothetical life cycle of a firm.

although an oversimplification, it provides a useful framework for analysis. The hypothesis is based upon a number of assumptions; it assumes competent management in the expansion period and insufficient management foresight prior to the decline phase. Obviously, one of management's primary goals is to prolong the growth phase and to avoid a decline completely. The great majority of firms achieve this by planning and control, which is the central contribution and responsibility of the finance function in a corporate structure.

Financial planning requires total integration and co-ordination of all the plans of the other functions of the firm. Financial planning therefore has to estimate the resources that will be required to carry out the operating plans and determine how far the resources can be generated by the firm itself and how far they will have to be obtained externally. A system of control on the other hand involves obtaining, processing and recording information in such a way that it can be easily analysed and thus highlight the areas in which improvements could be made to the operations of the firm.

Planning and control are thus obviously related. Planning is necessary to establish goals and standards. Control is necessary to obtain information promptly, to compare plans and performance, and to provide a feedback method whereby the system can be altered to improve performance.

2.2 THE NEED FOR CAPITAL

The foregoing is the barest summary of the finance function. A major task of financial management is the acquisition of funds at the lowest cost and under the best terms. Under conditions of perfect capital markets and certainty of supply of funds at all times, a financial manager would be able to pay out as dividends any cash on hand that was not required for the company's planned investment, and would be able to obtain any funds required for new investment at the precise moment that they were required, either by borrowing or by issuing new shares.

This is illustrated by a company's hypothetical cumulative financing requirement over a period of time, as shown in Figure 2.2. The cumulative

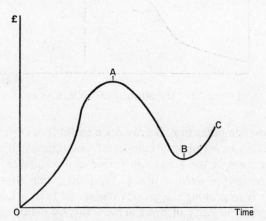

FIGURE 2.2. Cumulative financing requirement in a perfect capital market.

requirement is drawn upward sloping when the company is investing in new projects, and downward sloping when earnings are produced by those investments. Thus, in the example, during the time OA the company is investing greater amounts than those being earned from previous investments and it will therefore need to issue shares or borrow day by day throughout the period, in amounts just sufficient to keep up with the increasing financial requirement. Then in the period AB, the company will pay dividends day by day as its operations make the funds available. There is no need for the company to retain any of the funds made available because it is assumed that funds may be obtained instantaneously when required in the future. When the company undertakes new investment in the period BC, the cycle will be repeated.

Companies, however, do not operate in perfect capital markets. There is no certainty that funds will be available at the precise moment that they are required, and companies therefore have to carry stocks of capital to protect themselves from the vagaries of the market-place.

2.3 PERMANENT CAPITAL

2.31 Example of product life cycle cash flow

An important aspect of capital management is the recognition of cash flows over the life cycle of individual products. A new product or new firm typically experiences an initial period of cash flow deficits that must be financed from external sources. A typical product life cycle cash flow is described by Table 2.1 and Figure 2.3.

Table 2.1

PRODUCT LIFE CYCLE CASH FLOW

Year	Net Cash Flow	Cumulative Cash Flow
1974	(£ 3,000)	(£ 3,000)
1975	(17,000)	(20,000)
1976	(150,000)	(170,000)
1977	(30,000)	(200,000)
1978	20,000	(180,000)
1979	60,000	(120,000)
1980	110,000	(10,000)
1981	150,000	140,000
1982	180,000	320,000
1983	200,000	520,000
1984	200,000	720,000
1985	170,000	890,000
1986	120,000	1,010,000
1987	60,000	1,070,000
1988	30,000	1,100,000

Cash outflows are usually small while the firm undertakes the necessary market and related technological research to decide the feasibility of investing in a proposed product. Once the decision has been taken, however, cash outflows increase in size as investment in plant and machinery, stocks of raw materials, work in progress, and finished goods is undertaken before sales can be made. Sales will normally be made on credit terms and will thus produce trade debts which will result in additional time elapsing before a positive cash flow begins.

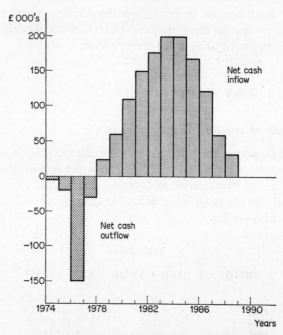

FIGURE 2.3.   Product life cycle cash flow.

The effect of such preparations is indicated in Table 2.1. After two years, when the preliminary stage has been completed, £20,000 has been spent. Engineering and manufacturing activities begin in 1976 and actual production and sales are started in 1977. Net cash flows are still negative at the end of 1977, at which time negative cash flows of £200,000 have been accumulated. This represents the amount that must be recognized as the total required investment by the company.

By 1978, positive cash flows begin. At first they are relatively small; then, as the firm captures a large share of the market, the cash flow increases. By 1980, positive cash flows are substantial and on a cumulative basis the total investment outlay has been recovered but for £10,000.

The success of the product, however, attracts other firms into the market. As a result, the originating firm's share of the market is squeezed, so that by the end of 1988 cash flows and related profits have declined to the point where serious consideration would be given to dropping the product.

The above example illustrates in broad outline the differing cash requirements associated with new product lines. The necessity of taking into consideration the heavy cash outlays required before commencing manufacturing is often underestimated. In addition, there is often insufficient recognition of the cash requirements needed to finance the investment in the initial work in progress, finished goods inventories, and debtors. The importance of a careful analysis of cash outflows in the set-up period cannot be emphasized too strongly if the firm is to avoid a cash crisis before positive cash flows begin.

2.32 Long-run cash flow cycle

The foregoing highlights the essential difference between capital and working capital management. The cycle described above consists of capital circulating into cash over a time interval long enough to permit the recovery of the cost of fixed assets, that is, the gradual recovery of original cash outlays on fixed assets through collections on sales, assuming prices cover costs, including depreciation. The problems posed are thus of a capital budgeting nature, which although concerned with the budgeting of funds primarily used for fixed assets, also requires budgeting for additions to working capital. This cash cycle is illustrated by Figure 2.4.

2.4 WORKING CAPITAL

Working capital management places even greater emphasis on the cash flow requirements of a company than that required under permanent capital management. Expanding companies require increasing investment in stocks, work in progress, and debtors as their scale of operations increases, until full capacity is reached. Then additional investment in fixed assets is required if growth is to continue. The interaction between working capital and sales is illustrated by the following example, and the results of the transactions are set out in Table 2.2.

2.41 Example of working capital management

1. Ten individuals each invest £1,000 in the Soft. S. Weter Co. Ltd. Plant and equipment is purchased for cash of £6,000 while cloth costs £3,000. The resulting financial situation is shown by Balance Sheet A.

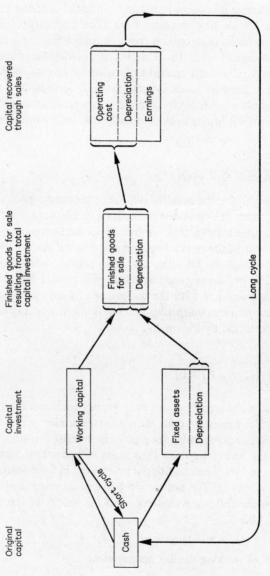

FIGURE 2.4. The long-run cash flow.

Table 2.2

SOFT. S. WETER CO. LTD.

Balance Sheet A

Capital	£10,000	Fixed Assets	
		Plant and Equipment	£6,000
		Current Assets	
		Stock	3,000
		Cash	1,000
	£10,000		£10,000

Balance Sheet B

Capital	£10,000	Fixed Assets	
		Plant and Equipment	6,000
Current Liabilities		Current Assets	
Creditors	5,000	Stock and work in progress	8,500
		Cash	500
	£15,000		£15,000

Balance Sheet C

Capital	£10,000	Fixed Assets	
Profit and Loss	1,020	Plant and Equipment	6,000
Current Liabilities		Current Assets	
Creditors	5,000	Stock and Work in Progress	3,400
		Debtors	6,120
		Cash	500
	£16,020		£16,020

Balance Sheet D

Capital	£10,000	Fixed Assets	
Profit and Loss	1,700	Plant and Equipment	6,000
		Current Assets	
		Cash	5,700
	£11,700		£11,700

2. Soft. S. Weter receives an order to manufacture 10,000 garments. The receipt of an order in itself has no effect on the balance sheet. However, in preparation for the manufacturing activity, the company buys £5,000 worth of cloth on terms of net 30 days. Without additional investment by the proprietors, total assets increase by £5,000 financed by the trade credit given by the supplier of the cloth. After the purchase, the company pays £500 to workers for cutting the cloth to the required pattern. The position is now as reflected in Balance Sheet B.

3. Soft. S. Weter delivers part (60%) of the original order, invoicing the purchaser for £6,120 payable within thirty days of date of invoice. The position is now as in Balance Sheet C, where it should be noted that stock and work in progress are replaced by debtors, the mark-up being reflected as retained earnings.

4. The remainder of the order is delivered, bringing total sales to £10,200. Balance Sheet D reflects the position once the company has received payment from the debtors and has extinguished its liability to the cloth supplier.

2.42   Short-run cash flow cycle

The idea of the short-run cash cycle can now be generalized. An order that requires the purchase of raw materials is placed with the firm, which in its turn generates a creditor. The raw materials are processed, thus giving rise to work in progress until the articles are completed, when stocks of finished goods are held. The articles are sold on credit thereby giving rise to debtors. As the company has not received cash, this point in the cycle represents the peak financing requirement. As debtors settle their accounts cash becomes available with which short-term creditors can be paid. The cycle is summarized in Figure 2.5.

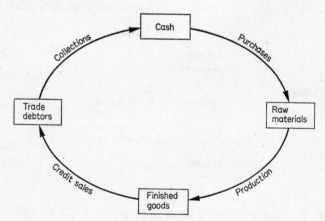

FIGURE 2.5.   The short-run cash flow.

2.43   Fluctuating versus permanent assets

The influence of sales on current asset levels is illustrated above. Over the course of several cycles, fluctuations in sales will be accompanied in most industries by a rising long-term trend. Figure 2.6 shows the consequences

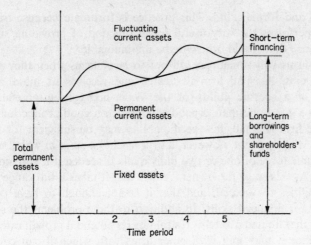

FIGURE 2.6. Fluctuating versus permanent assets.

of such a pattern. Total permanent assets increase steadily in the form of current and fixed assets. Increases of this nature should be financed by long-term borrowings or additional permanent capital; temporary increases in assets can be covered by increasing short-term liabilities.

The distinction between temporary and permanent asset levels may be difficult to make in practice, but it is neither illusory nor unimportant. Short-term financing of long-term needs is dangerous. A profitable firm may become unable to meet its cash obligations if funds borrowed on a short-term basis have become tied up in permanent assets.

2.5 EXPERTISE AVAILABLE FROM THE FACTOR

2.51 Financing requirements of a firm

A relationship exists between a firm's growth in sales and the nature of its financing requirements. The small, successful firm will typically have a high sales growth rate, 30 to 50 per cent a year. Profits as a percentage of sales will be somewhat higher than the average for large manufacturing companies but compared with traditional and customary standards, its financial position is relatively weak. A high return on net worth is normally indicated and this further underlines the firm's precarious financial position.

Studies of new, small firms indicate that 80 per cent to 90 per cent of the initial financing comes from the funds of the owners of the business, and their relatives and friends. As sales grow, the major initial source of external financing is likely to be trade credit. Suppliers provide credit of both an informal and formal kind. This practice is fortunate because trade credit thereby performs the very useful social function of providing small firms with finance that would otherwise be unobtainable.

Small firms will sometimes sell out to large firms when they grow to a certain point. A small firm is created and receives its initial impulsion because of a specific ability of the owner-manager-entrepreneur. He is probably a good salesman, a good engineer, or a good production man and while the firm is small, his specific ability may be sufficient for the firm's success. At some point, however, a firm reaches a stage at which more than the dynamic force of one or two individuals is needed if it is to continue to prosper. At this stage the owners realize that it takes a full range of managerial abilities to succeed, and that it is not enough to have only sales, technical, or financial skills. In addition to these problems the small firm may find that limited capital is restraining its potential growth rate, and as a consequence it may join with other firms with which it can complement strengths and weaknesses.

The firm that progresses beyond this stage as an independent entity to become a medium-sized firm will probably experience growth rates and profit rates lower than those for the new, small firm. The medium firm will be in a somewhat better financial position because it will by definition have been in operation long enough to have established a performance record that gives it at least a degree of access to external funds. Such a firm will probably have a need to finance further growth, but if the necessary funds are denied by outside parties then it could be forced to seek a merger with another firm, in order to compete effectively with its larger competitors.

2.52   How the factor can assist

Whatever the size of the firm and the stage of its development, a system of financial planning and control appropriate to its circumstances is essential if growth is to be achieved with the minimum of risks. While the factor does not seek to play any part in the management of client companies, expertise can be offered to clients on request outside the normal service areas of collection, credit protection, and accounting of trade debts. The factor can highlight weaknesses in a client's system of financial planning and control, particularly in the area of working capital management and the flow of short-term funds, and can suggest possible improvements.

While such advice can greatly benefit the client, the major financial advantage of a factoring facility is certainty in cash flow. The factor undertakes to pay at clearly defined points in time an agreed percentage in respect of invoices offered by the client, such payment not being subject to a facility limit, as is the case with a bank overdraft for example. The client is thus assured that as his turnover increases, the financial availability from the factor will increase in direct proportion.

From the factor's viewpoint, a relationship with a client has been successful when a period of growth has been sustained in a controlled manner, and when the client's financial strength is such that the company's access to other forms of external funds is made easier.

3   The Scope of Factoring

3.1   THE IMPORTANCE OF INTERNATIONAL TRADE IN THE DEVELOPMENT OF FACTORING

The historical development of the present-day factor is not only interesting in itself but allows evaluation of the true relationship between factoring and its close ties with international trade. Although factoring is a fairly recent management and financial instrument in the United Kingdom, having been established since the early 1960s, it nevertheless dates back to the Middle Ages, when the factor carried out what was essentially a marketing function. The problems resulting from rudimentary transportation and communications meant that the development of a domestic market, even more an international market, was a hazardous operation.

3.11   Early marketing function of the factor

The factor developed from the Middle Ages onwards concurrently with international trade. The expansion of the English cloth industry in the fourteenth and fifteenth centuries, enjoying a bountiful supply of raw materials on which heavy export duties were levied, and an abundance of necessary water power, led to the increased importance of the English merchant in European trade. Documents of the period relating to the expanding English cloth trade show the extended use of credit in dealings between buyer and seller. The manufacturer or local merchant found it convenient to ship merchandise to the factor who would act as a commission agent, taking goods on a consignment basis, selling those goods in his locality, and carrying out collections for the seller. For these functions, namely selling, maintaining a form of sales ledger, and collection, the factor would receive a commission. He would also give advice as to the suitability of merchandise for his local market.

3.12   Growth of the financial function

It is in the marketing capacity that factors first contributed to the growth of international trade. They are often referred to from the Middle Ages onwards, and their importance grew from the fourteenth century. The financial services associated with present-day factoring arose naturally from the original marketing functions. It was natural that the factor should not only advise upon the creditworthiness of the individual customers to whom he was selling on behalf of the supplier, but also, for an additional fee, guarantee the supplier as to the buyer's ability to pay. He was acting as a *del credere* agent in this situation and built up a fund of credit knowledge, particularly from current dealings with a number of buyers. As he was controlling the various book debts that he was generating on behalf of the manufacturer and had good knowledge of the expectation of payment from customers, it became possible for him to make advance payments to the manufacturer in anticipation of receipts from debtors. This eased the financial burden upon the supplier through the manufacturing, shipment, selling, and collection period.

The factor usually retained a percentage of debts generated to all customers to allow for settlement of disputes, which he dealt with on the supplier's behalf and with his consent. Eventually, due to the seasonal nature of certain trades, the factor assisted the supplier in making advances when required on merchandise shipped to, and in the possession of, the factor. It is clear that at this point the factor was looked to by the supplier for marketing and financial functions.

3.2 THE AMERICAN EXPERIENCE

The transformation of the factor, from performing the dual function of marketing and credit control to concentration on credit control and financial activities alone, occurred in America. The factor is found in the earliest records of trade between England and America. The Plymouth Colony established partnerships to deal in imports of products such as shoes, cotton and woollen cloth, and tools. In turn these sent primary products such as furs, fish, and timber to London merchants, referred to as 'agents and factors', to sell on their behalf.

3.21 The cloth trade, and the extension of factoring

The extension of the cloth trade from England to America in the eighteenth and nineteenth centuries brought with it the strengthening of the factor's position in servicing American imports of English manufactured products. While the factor was still found in England, the services of the factor were more in demand in America for a variety of reasons. The great distance between markets gave rise to an automatic demand for the factor's service for both American and English imports. More particularly, the continual westward expansion of the American market, especially from the beginning of the nineteenth century, added to its vast physical range, made it extraordinarily difficult for the English supplier to operate without either a local sales and collection agent, or advice on and, more usefully, protection against credit risks arising from sales to individual buyers. Moreover, the lag between production and final payment from customers meant that the supplier turned to the factor for financial assistance.

As the American economy developed from a primary to a secondary economic situation, development of natural resources was undertaken to supply a growing domestic market. The American textile industry, aided by the advantages of differential freight charges for delivery to the domestic user, presented an automatic challenge to the English cloth exporter. Added to this, increased tariff barriers assisted the emergent domestic American industry, so that individual units could realize economies of scale and compete on a more than equal basis. In the late nineteenth century dramatic changes in the pattern of trade occurred, with the American producer supplanting the English mill as the major supplier to the American textile market.

'Between 1889 and 1905, the selling functions of the factoring houses gradually disappeared and the factor became a specialized banker. The McKinley tariff of 1890 practically forced European textiles out of the American market and the factoring houses naturally turned to American mills and converters, for whom they performed the same financial services they had been providing to the European mills, but as the American mills had their own sales departments, there was no occasion for the factor to act in a selling capacity.'*

3.22 Change in the nature of factoring

Faced with this situation, the American factor fashioned his services to suit the requirements of the emergent American textile mill. Unlike the English exporter, the American producer was concerned to establish direct marketing links with his customers and the factor dropped his marketing function but continued to offer:

(*a*) credit control and protection against bad debts,

(*b*) detailed sales ledgering,

(*c*) collection of all debts from individual customers,

(*d*) financing of debts where required.

* R. I. Livingston, 'Assignment of Accounts Receivable', *Illinois Bar Journal*, Vol. 42 pp. 773, 774 (Supplement 1954).

Although parting with control of the merchandise, the factor nevertheless controlled collections on a direct basis. The buyer was informed that the debt had been purchased by and was payable to the factor by a notation on the invoice. Factoring services were of importance to the American producer wishing to concentrate on production and marketing, and to avoid bad debts or liquidity problems in a period of intensive growth.

Table 3.1

UNITED STATES GROSS NATIONAL PRODUCT and FACTORING VOLUME 1940–1972
(figures in thousand million dollars)

Year	U.S.A. Gross National Product*	U.S.A. Factoring Volume
1940	99·7	0·79
1941	125·8	1·14
1942	159·1	1·44
1943	192·5	1·49
1944	211·4	1·50
1945	213·6	1·56
1946	210·7	2·41
1947	234·3	2·43
1948	259·4	2·49
1949	258·1	2·10
1950	284·6	2·70
1951	329·0	2·80
1952	347·0	3·10
1953	365·4	3·10
1954	363·1	3·15
1955	398·0	3·70
1956	419·2	4·30
1957	440·3	4·50
1958	444·5	4·14
1959	482·7	4·68
1960	502·6	4·91
1961	518·2	4·91
1962	554·9	5·40
1963	583·9	5·50
1964	632·4	6·11
1965	683·9	6·66
1966	743·3	7·39
1967	789·7	7·83
1968	846·2	8·77
1969	929·1	9·47
1970	974·1	10·13
1971	1,050·4	13·31
1972	1,150·5	14·66

* Figures for States of Alaska and Hawaii are included after 1960.

Sources: 1. National Commercial Finance Conference, Inc.
            (estimates of member companies volumes)
          2. Statistical Abstract of the United States.

3.23 The twentieth century

The twentieth century saw the expansion of factoring away from the textile industry to other areas where the expertise of credit checking and protection against bad debts, ledgering and collection, and receivables financing could be applied. Consumer products such as shoes, toys, furniture, and hats were obvious choices, as were the new and developing industries of electronics, chemicals, and synthetic fibres, where once again manufacturers were keen to develop quickly without liquidity or bad debt problems.

Total sales factored are estimated to have reached $500 million by the early 1930s and Table 3.1 shows that a volume exceeding $1,000 million was achieved by 1941. From 1946 to 1970 sales factored held fairly closely to 1 per cent of Gross National Product, but moved significantly higher thereafter suggesting an upward shift from the plateau of penetration achieved in the twenty-five years following World War II. By the mid-twentieth century the American factoring industry, with its origins in international trade, looked abroad. If the techniques of factoring were useful domestically, why not in world markets in order to service open credit transactions between those markets?

3.3 DEVELOPMENT OF FACTORING IN THE UNITED KINGDOM

The factor has remained close to his original origins in performing the marketing function in the English market, eventually acting as distributor to many trades. Today motor accessories, electrical products, and other distributive industries are ones where factors are found acting in a merchanting capacity.

3.31 Characteristics of British factoring

The financial factor started to develop in the late 1950s, and American influence was significant either in direct equity participation or strong management links and advice. In general British factors were based on the American model of purchasing debts without recourse to the client in the event of customer failure to pay, and performance of the ledgering and collection functions. There were however one or two exceptions where all services were offered except protection against bad debts. While large institutions were involved in the formation of factoring houses the absence of the major clearing banks was noticeable.

The early 1960s ushered in a period of severe credit squeeze and this, coinciding with the establishment of many factoring companies, led to factoring being used by many clients purely as an alternative source to bank finance with an almost complete disregard of the services offered in a true factoring facility. The factors built up their local expertise slowly and nearly all had a chequered start, selectivity of clients being enforced only gradually. Sales factored per annum by the mid 1960s were in the region of £100 million, but the optimistic forecasts of a figure of £1,000 million by the early 1970s have not been achieved.

Nevertheless, the 1960s have seen the establishment of the British factoring industry on a solid basis. Many unsuitable clients ceased to factor and, ironically, the easing of credit controls, which spelt more competition for the factoring industry, may well have led to the direct involvement of all major clearing banks in factoring, in an attempt to broaden the base of their financial services to industry. Coinciding with this development was the increasing involvement of American banks, and the years 1970 and 1971 saw the addition of five new factoring companies although two were to merge into larger groupings. Table 3.2 shows clearly the two periods of enlargement of the industry, namely the mid 1960s and 1970/1971.

3.32 Parallel development of banking and factoring in America

It is interesting to note the parallel development in the twentieth century in America of several commercial banks offering a factoring service. This trend was extremely clear in the late 1960s, when the American banks opened factoring departments or acquired operating factors. In 1968 the First Pennsylvania Banking and Trust Company set up its own factoring division. Within a few years a number of factors were purchased, the factoring houses of Coleman and Company, Shapiro Brothers Factors Corporation, Congress Factors Corporation, and L. F. Dommerich and Company Inc., all being acquired by banks. The increasing involvement of the American banks in factoring, from 1968 onwards, is clearly shown in Table 3.3. Where purchases have occurred it is interesting to note that management of the factor has not been merged with that of the bank, the different attitudes necessary for banking and factoring being recognized by operating separate personnel.

3.33 The 1970s in Britain

In the United Kingdom the early 1970s saw the emphasis placed on the service aspect of factoring, a generally higher quality of client, and a greater acceptance of factoring throughout the business community wherever the

Table 3.2 THE MAJOR U.K. FACTORING COMPANIES

Company	Year Incorporated	Shareholders	Size of Holding (%)	Issued Capital	Primarily With or Without Recourse	Method of International Operations
Alex Lawrie Factors Ltd., Dunster House, 17-20 Mark Lane, London EC3R 7BY.	1962	Alex Lawrie Holdings Ltd. (in turn 72% owned by Walter Duncan Goodricke Ltd, Minority shareholders Banque Belge Ltd, 20%; Mr. N. A. Grant, 8%).	100	£1,000,000	With recourse	Member of Factors Chain International.
Arbuthnot Factors Ltd., Arbuthnot House, Breeds Place, Hastings, Sussex TN34 3AB.	1964	Arbuthnot Latham Holdings Ltd.	100	£500,000	Without recourse	Member of Factors Chain International.
BankAmerica—Williams Glyn Factors Ltd., Rothschild House, Whitgift Centre, Croydon CR9 3RE.	1970	Bamerical International Financial Corporation Williams & Glyn's Bank Mr. J. K. Holland	51 39 10	£441,176	Without recourse	Through Bank of America banking offices.
Barclays Factoring (Part of Barclays Export & Finance Co. Ltd.), P.O. Box No. 9, Paddington House Town Centre, Basingstoke RG21 1BE	1964 (commenced 1971)	Barclays Bank Ltd.	100	£5,000,000	Without recourse	Full international factoring services not yet provided. Alternative services available.

Company	Established	Owned by	%	Capital	Recourse	Network
Credit Factoring International Ltd., Smith House, P.O. Box 50, Elmwood Avenue, Feltham, Middx. TW13 7QD.	1970	National Westminster	100	£1,000,000	Without recourse	Own network of overseas offices.
Griffin Factors Ltd., Plantation House, Mincing Lane, London EC3M 3LE.	1963	Midland Bank Finance Corporation Ltd.	100	£1,000,000	Without recourse	Member of Factors Chain International.
H & H Factors Ltd., Randolph House, 46–68 Wellesley Road, Croydon, Surrey CR9 3PS.	1964	Walter E. Heller Overseas Corp. / Hambros Bank Ltd. / Continental Illinois National Bank & Trust Co. of Chicago / Keep Bros. Ltd., / Others	63 / 25 / 10 / 1 / 1	£1,250,000	Without recourse	Member of Walter E. Heller International factoring network.
International Factors Ltd., Circus House, New England Road, Brighton BN1 4EX.	1960	Lloyds & Scottish Finance / First National Bank of Boston	75 / 25	£1,000,000	Without recourse	Part of International Factors network of Associate Companies.
Factoring Division of Mercantile Credit Co. Ltd., P.O. Box 75, Elizabethan House, Great Queen Street, London WC2B 5DP.	1934 (commenced factoring 1965)	Public Company	Public Company	£23,923,655	With recourse	Reciprocal collection arrangements with European Finance Companies.

Source: Individual factors listed

Table 3.3   INVOLVEMENT OF U.S. BANKS IN FACTORING

Bank	Factor	Year founded	Method
Bank of America	Own factor or division	1937	Own office
Trust Company of Georgia	Own factor or division	1939	Own office
First National Bank of Boston	Own factor or division	1945	Own office
First National City Corporation (New York)	Hubshman Factors Corp.	1965	By acquisition
Citizens & Southern National Bank (Atlanta)	Joel Hurt Factors Inc.	1965	By acquisition
United California Bank (L.A.)	Atlas Factors Inc.	1966	By acquisition
United California Bank (L.A.)	Produce Clearings Inc.	1966	By acquisition
Philadelphia National Bank	Congress Factors	1967	By acquisition
Fidelity Bank, Philadelphia	John P. Maguire Co.	1967	Working agreement (bank provides funds, factor provides service)
Marine Midland Banks of N.Y.	John P. Maguire Co.	N/A	Working agreement (bank provides funds, factor provides service)
First Pennsylvania Banking & Trust Co.	Own factor or division	1968	Own office
National Network & Essex Bank	National Business Credit	1968	By acquisition
Bankers Trust New York Corporation	Coleman & Co.	1968	By acquisition
Chase Manhattan Bank, New York	Shapiro Bros. Factors	1968	By acquisition
Chemical Bank, New York	L. F. Dommerich & Co.	1968	By acquisition
Bank of Commerce, New York	Milberg Factors	1968	Working agreement (bank provides funds, factor provides service)

Bank	Factor	Year	Method
Morris Plan Company of California	Business Factors Inc.	1968	By acquisition
Union County Trust Co., New Jersey	Milberg Factors	1968	Working agreement (bank provides funds, factor provides service)
First Union National Bank of N.C. (Charlotte)	H. A. Caesar	1969	By acquisition
Virginia Commonwealth Bankshares (Richmond)	Rusch Factors	1969	By acquisition
Wachovia Bank & Trust Co., N.C.	Southeastern Financial Corp.	1969	By acquisition (being challenged by Justice Department)
First National Bank, Atlanta	Walter E. Heller & Co.	1969	Joint venture (separate corporation formed and partners continue existing activities)
Liberty National Bank, Oklahoma City	Walter E. Heller & Co.	1969	Joint venture (separate corporation formed and partners continue existing activities)
North Carolina National Bank	Factors Inc.	1970	By acquisition
Central National Bank, Chicago	Rawleigh Moses & Company	1970	By acquisition
Chase Manhattan Bank, New York	Interstate Factors Corp.	1970	By acquisition
Virginia Commonwealth Bankshares	Canadian Factors Corp.	1971	By acquisition
First National Bank in Dallas	Lane Wood & Co.	1971	By acquisition
Industrial National Bank of R.I. (Providence)	Ambassador Factors	1972	By acquisition
Provident National Bank (Philadelphia)	John P. Maguire & Co.	1972	By acquisition
Manufacturers Hanover Corporation	Iselin-Jefferson Finance Co. Inc.	1972	By acquisition
United Virginia Bank	Crompton-Richmond Co. Factors	1972	By acquisition
Fidelity Corporation of America	Commercial Capital Corporation	1973	By acquisition
Mid City National Bank of Chicago	Iroquois Company	1973	By acquisition
Marine Midland Bank, N.Y.	AIC Financial Corporation	1974	By acquisition

techniques can be applied. The restricting historical association with textiles is not in evidence, although textiles remain an area suited to the application of factoring techniques. By the end of 1974 total sales factored per annum approached a rate of £500 million and this figure is expected to grow considerably under the stimulus of clearing bank involvement, European Common Market trade on an open credit basis, and increasing sophistication of factoring services and the marketing of factoring as a whole. Certainly the penetration of the factoring industry in the United Kingdom, which by 1974 had reached 0·5 per cent of Gross National Product, suggests that factoring as a whole has yet to realize its full potential when compared to the American situation.

3.34 Increased involvement of banking institutions

Finally, a degree of rationalisation has emphasized the increased involvement of banking institutions, not by way of purchase of factoring companies by the banks or the bank factors, but rather by reduction in the number of factoring companies not having a bank as a controlling shareholder. In 1972 the continuing factoring business of Allied Factors Limited was acquired by H & H Factors Limited and this was followed in 1973 by the merger of Midland Citibank Factors and Shield Factors Limited (now Griffin Factors Limited), and the purchase of Bankers Trust Factors Limited by Alex Lawrie Factors Limited.

3.4 APPLICATION OF FACTORING

The historical development of factoring traces a rapid movement away from the textile industry, once it was realized that the techniques involved were capable of universal application. However, there are certain questions that must be answered satisfactorily before the factor will offer a facility.

3.41 Is the debt security sufficient?

Factors generally desire to offer protection against bad debts arising from individual customer's inability to pay. In this way the client's net worth and profit position will not be prejudiced in the event of customer failure, and therefore the client need not be viewed from a pure lending position. Provided that the factor has purchased a bona fide and collectable debt from the client, without recourse to the client, the factor is looking to his own ability to collect on that security and can expand his facility with the client's growth. Any 'financing' of trade debts, by advancing an agreed percentage prior to settlement date, occurs not by way of loan, nor with any contingent liability, but by the payment by the factor for assets purchased. For the factor to view the facility as a 'non-lending' operation it is essential that he can rely on the debt security, or realizability of assets (trade debts), without reference to the client.

Certain industries present many problems for the factor. For example, he is unable to purchase progress invoices covering part of an overall contract and sustain his debt security in many situations. A part-finished heating installation, engine, road, or factory is of no use to the buyer if the seller (the factor's client) cannot complete the contract. The buyer's refusal to pay for invoices validly raised in accordance with the contract and held by the factor is understandable as the contract must now be finished usually at much higher cost and at a later date. This incurs loss to the buyer, and the factor will find that consequent non-payment of invoices held can cause considerable loss.

It is not usual, therefore, to find factoring applied to the building and certain engineering industries where the problems of realizability occur. The reserve withheld by the factor when advancing funds against invoices purchased is to allow for normal contingencies of returns or disputes, and not for heavy contractual offset situations.

3.42 Can the factoring services be applied in a proper manner?

A worthwhile relationship cannot develop between the factor and his client unless the client is in an industry and situation where the factoring service can be applied properly. The factor is initially appraising the client's stated plans for development and relating these to the tools at hand, namely the management, financial resources, production and marketing capability of the client. Within this context the factor must relate the need for his services and his ability to fulfil the requirements of the client.

CREDIT INVESTIGATION AND PROTECTION

The factor will investigate large credit risk concentrations, the general credit standing of the client's major customers, and the general category of debtors arising from the prospective client's operations. It is rare for a factor to be involved with sales other than to the industrial and commercial sectors. The factor will draw on various sources of credit information and his record of dealing with industry and commerce in approving credit sales. This is not available to him in the personal sector. If the factor, as is usual, wishes to perform the full service of factoring, including protection against bad debts for the client, then he will not wish to offer a facility where he cannot countenance the major customer risks or have access to meaningful credit information.

COLLECTION PROCEDURES

Collection must also be undertaken by the factor as a general rule without reference to the client. This does not mean that the factor will exclude the client totally from all aspects of collection, and factors differ as to their approach on this point. Legally it is true that the factor can proceed in all aspects of collection without reference to the client, but continuing goodwill must be taken into account and some client-factor co-operation may exist in this sphere. However, if a factor has to ask for the client's assistance on a general basis for routine collection matters, it is clear that the client is paying for a service that in this case does not exist. The managing director of an engineering company that has to negotiate payments on account of contracts under completion with his various customers, in order that the factor should receive payment, is not deriving full benefit from the factor's services. The inability of the factor to conduct routine collection procedures tends to arise in those industries where the general problems of debt security or realizability arise.

REVIEW OF CLIENT'S FINANCIAL REQUIREMENTS

Finally the factor will review the financial requirements of the client in achieving his stated objectives. The financial effect of a factoring facility, if payments are being made against invoices prior to due date of settlement, is to reduce the debtor item. A loan is not created, and the use of increased velocity of working capital will be considered. The factor will enquire as to the gross profit margin of additional sales now possible, whether the client has reached or will reach and pass break-even point, and what return on capital employed can now be achieved. He will also look closely at the ability of management to reach the increased volume of sales envisaged.

Only if these questions are answered satisfactorily will a facility be offered to a prospective client.

3.43   Will the facility be profitable for both parties?

While it is for the client to judge whether he should enter the factoring contract, it is for the factor to decide whether the contract should be offered, and at what rates. Generally a charge of between $\frac{3}{4}$ per cent and 2 per cent of sales will be made for the services of credit investigation and protection, ledgering, and collection. A further charge would be made on moneys advanced prior to settlement date at a rate equivalent to or slightly in excess of that charged by a bank for overdraft facilities.

In estimating profitability the factor will be looking to the total sales factored per annum and the workload constituting such sales. Any facility will require a certain degree of executive time, individual control, and proper supervision. For this reason the factor will generally require a minimum sales figure of £100,000 per annum for each client.

Similarly the factor will be concerned with the average value of invoices, number of active customers, and continuity of trading with those customers. Invoice values of less than £50 are rarely contemplated, while clients dealing in 'one off' transactions with customers involve a heavy workload. The average collection period and any unusual terms of payment are also investigated. A very long collection period and unusual payment terms normally require more work for the factor's collection department.

Clients whose sales are less than £100,000 per annum, with average invoice value below £50, and with many customers in relation to total sales, can expect a factoring service charge well in excess of 2 per cent of sales, if a facility is offered at all.

The factor is also concerned as to the profitable use of the facility by the client. The client using factoring as a financial line of last resort is, in many cases, only postponing the end, and the factor will find that much time and effort has to be devoted to such situations. Similarly a client entering a factoring contract for a very marginal financial benefit would not develop a long-term association of real worth to both parties. The factor therefore, for reasons of self-interest, is concerned that his services are put to proper and profitable use by the client, as only in this way will a profitable portfolio of clients emerge.

4 The Need for Factoring

4.1 THE ECONOMIC FUNCTION OF FACTORING

An analysis of the economic function of factoring must be conducted at two levels, that of the economy as a whole and that of the individual firm.

4.11 Factoring and the national economy

FINANCIAL EFFECTS

At present the financial effect of factoring related to the national economy is very small. The rate of total sales factored per annum approached £500 million by the end of 1974. This represents approximately half of 1 per cent of Gross National Product and is equivalent to an approximate figure of debtors outstanding at any time of £100 million. Because factors hold a contingencies reserve of between 20 per cent and 25 per cent on average, excluding those accounts where the factor is not carrying out any financing prior to settlement date, this represents a maximum investment by the factoring industry of approximately £75 million at any one time. This figure can be compared with bank credit extended throughout the economy well in excess of £10,000 million and industrial trade credit which is far in excess of total bank credit.

ECONOMIC EFFECTS

It is therefore clear that the financial effects of factoring on the economy as a whole are still fairly insignificant. Nevertheless, in an economic sense factoring is important because it operates at the margin of industrial organization, and in any event its activity should grow so that the general economic effects of factoring are an important consideration. Moreover, many of the economic effects are concerned with the services offered by the factor rather than the financial 'investment' of the factoring industry.

SHIFTING OF RESOURCES

The points covered in this section relate to an economy working within the concept of the price mechanism, allowing allocation of resources according to supply and demand. The resources of land, labour, capital, and organization allow for the production of goods and services to satisfy consumer requirements. These resources will be shifted according to shifting demand patterns, both domestic and international. In an economy assuming complete knowledge and immediate mobility and control of resources, demand patterns cause shifts in allocation of resources to maximize the satisfaction of consumers. In practice this does not happen, as there are imperfections distorting this mechanism. Nevertheless, over the medium or long term, continual adjustment is occurring as investment, production, and marketing decisions are made in relation to anticipated medium- and long-term demand patterns.

Limiting factors in the shifting of resources are management and finance, and in both of these areas factoring can be of assistance. Every economy has limited resources in relation to the demands of its individuals. To satisfy wants by producing one product, factors of production must be diverted from producing other products. This is the real opportunity cost of the articles produced. To complicate the position demand is continually shifting and this in turn causes reactions in production, but again this only occurs through time.

EFFECT ON CONTROL OVER RESOURCES

Factoring assists this process in allowing a faster reaction to changes in demand by aiding dynamic, efficient firms with lower costs of production to adjust their output more quickly. The factor is able to permit greater expansion by the more efficient firm from an existing capital base and can also allow management problems to be contained during a growth period. In assisting those firms operating in expanding sectors of the economy, or those firms that are more efficient and therefore have lower cost curves than their competitors, the factor is allowing these areas of the economy to obtain control over existing resources. This control is required in order to satisfy changing consumer wants on a more efficient and shorter time-scale.

Therefore from any given set of factors of production a greater output of goods and services is possible, and it is probable that they will be produced more closely in line with consumer demands than would otherwise be the case. If we introduce value judgments into this argument and state that growth and the maximum possible satisfaction of consumer wants is a good objective, then we can say that factoring assists in the attainment of that objective.

USE OF SPECIALIZED RESOURCES BY THE FACTOR

The preceding argument has been concerned with the ability of the efficient firm to obtain the resources necessary for expansion of output at known cost. A reduction in costs per unit of output may also occur as factoring allows the application of the principle of division of labour in certain areas. Specialized resources can be used to carry out certain management functions. The appendix to this chapter (*see* page 43) shows, with the use of diagrams found in many standard economics textbooks, the effects of factoring upon output, cost, and price for the individual firm and the industry within which it operates.

By applying his services to a large number of clients the factor is able to engage specialists in the areas of credit protection, accounting, and collection and apply those specialists to the number of clients that is relevant, bearing in mind the workload for each client. The factor is therefore able to employ specialized factors of production in relation to sales ledger control and to overcome the problem of indivisibility of resources. For example, whereas the company with a sales turnover of £400,000 per annum could not afford the services of a highly-skilled credit controller, an accountant, or a skilled collection man in order to keep day-to-day control of its sales ledger, it can obtain the services of these personnel through the factoring facility. The factor engaging a credit assessor or credit man at £3,500 per annum can use so much of the credit assessor's time at that level of decision-making necessary for the client. A client with 500 customers may require some ten per cent of the time of the credit assessor at a high level of decision-making, and therefore the credit assessor can be 'applied' to ten such clients.

More Efficient Allocation of Time

This principle can be used throughout the functions undertaken by the factor and as the workload over various functions can vary within each client facility, so the factor can employ more or less time of its individual specialists. For instance, the same client may be in an industry where fairly long credit is taken, so that more collection time is undertaken for the client and a collection manager may only be able to spread his services over five such clients. In effect this means that management decisions in relation to sales ledger control are being made by personnel most suited to those decisions, and those personnel are engaged fully throughout the operation.

Compared to this situation the individual company, without the factoring service, may have to employ one fairly senior accountant or credit controller to perform all functions relating to sales ledger control. At certain times this will mean that highly-skilled resources of management are being used at fairly low levels of decision-making. Alternatively the client will hire staff appropriate to a much lower level of decision-making, so that either inefficiency will result in that section of the company or senior management will be involved in mundane decisions, which once again will cause operating inefficiency.

DEVELOPMENT OF THE ENTREPRENEURIAL FUNCTION

The factor, therefore, is able to assist in a more efficient use of resources and in the adjustment of supply to demand patterns. Assistance can also be given to the major dynamic area in any economy, namely the development of the entrepreneurial function. The entrepreneurial function is concerned with the organization of factors of production to allow goods and services to be produced in relation to anticipated demands. The entrepreneur is concerned with the minimization of risk in estimating the demand for future goods and services, and in estimating the results of the decision to allocate resources to satisfy such a demand.

In many cases there will be a need to employ market research organizations in order to attempt to define the market for the product. The factor can assist in estimating the supply or cost function by minimizing the possibility of bad debt risk inherent in the future supply of goods and services and the uncertainty as to receipts from individual debtors; and finally in reducing overhead costings for certain functions carried out by the factor to a known figure in relation to sales.

4.12   Factoring and the individual firm

The prime economic function of the factor in relation to the individual firm is to relieve the constraints placed upon the firm by the 'imperfect' state of the real world. Following upon the value judgment that the satisfaction of consumer wants is a good objective, the economist will analyze the optimum allocation of resources according to demand by assuming a position of perfect knowledge, mobility of resources, and organizational ability. The fact that this is not so does not detract from the analytical usefulness of the economic models produced from such assumptions. However, it is clear that the individual firm does suffer many real constraints, some of which the factor can assist in overcoming.

FINANCIAL CONSTRAINT

Even with sophisticated marketing methods and production planning, it is still not possible to determine the exact result of investment and marketing decisions. The industrialist may be assisted by market research, operational research, and complex financial analysis to analyze present day rates of return on investment projects. Yet a decision on allocation of production resources must still be taken without full knowledge of actual demand curves or functions (quantities demanded at different prices) or indeed of macro-economic developments that may have a direct effect. For example, a change in government policy, such as increasing deposits under hire purchase contracts, will affect demand for goods sold on a hire purchase basis. This means that the raising of equity capital becomes more difficult either privately or from the public market. Risk becomes a real factor as the return on additional investment must be discounted for uncertainty. For the smaller company this could mean that it is unable to continue profitable expansion.

While factoring is not an alternative to raising long-term capital, it can be of real assistance in increasing the velocity of working capital, often a necessary partner to any increase in long-term capital if the overall financial plan for the company is to be achieved. The traditional flow of working capital from stock into production, and then into trade debts which are eventually returned to the company as cash, is shortened as payments are made against invoices purchased. To an agreed extent the debtor item is transformed into cash for the client. Expansion is not restricted due to lack of working capital and can occur to meet customer demand.

MANAGEMENT CONSTRAINT

In the growth of every company there comes a point where existing management resources are insufficient to sustain an efficient growth situation, that is to say an extension along the lowest possible cost curve of that company. Many companies are often started by a production- or marketing-orientated entrepreneur, and credit control and financial management are not given primary attention. This often leads to inefficient utilization of working capital and the undertaking of credit risks on a haphazard basis.

By utilizing a factoring facility the company has recourse to increased management ability in the specialized spheres of credit management, covering efficient credit control and protection, ledgering, and detailed collection. As the company grows, so the factor will allocate more specialized personnel to the problems posed in the credit, accounting, and collection areas. In this sphere, therefore, the firm can expand without the normal management constraints.

DIVISION OF LABOUR AND ECONOMIES OF SCALE CONSTRAINT

The use of a factoring facility by the growing company also allows that company to enjoy economies of scale in the credit control area that are out of relation to its present size. Table 4.1 shows how the principle of division

Table 4.1

COMPARATIVE STAFF COSTS and UTILIZATION

(a) *Client operating own sales ledger*

	£ per annum
1 Credit/Collection/Accounts Controller	2,500
1 Accounts Clerk	1,000
	£3,500

Excess capacity from time to time

(b) *Factor operating the client sales ledger*

	£ cost per annum	% of time used	£ per annum
1 Credit Controller	3,500	20	700
1 Collection Specialist	2,500	20	500
1 Accounts Clerk	1,200	$33\frac{1}{3}$	400
1 Accounts Controller	3,200	$12\frac{1}{2}$	400
Sundry staff allocation			500
			£2,500

No excess capacity

of labour and specialization of resources can be applied, so that the factor can employ specialists for the client at a higher remuneration, but at a lower total cost. The specialization by the factor, and its application of those resources over many clients, allows the principle of division of labour to operate for its individual clients.

PREDICTION CONSTRAINT

One of the problems of taking management decisions is that their results cannot be foreseen with accuracy. Just as the market research firm is useful to the decision-maker in minimizing the uncertainty in estimating the demand curve for a product, so the factor can minimize the uncertainty surrounding the effect on working capital of expansion plans.

If a maturity factoring arrangement is employed, the functions of credit control and protection, ledgering, and collection being undertaken by the factor with a guaranteed payment of trade debts on an agreed maturity date, the manager can, in planning growth, complete his cash flow as to receipts from debtors with far greater certainty. He can also judge his working capital requirements with less need for a cash float for unforeseen contingencies.

With an 'old line' factoring service, a 'maturity' factoring facility with agreed immediate availability of payment against invoices factored, the total working capital requirement is reduced dramatically as the manager can plan upon receipts of up to 80 per cent from 'debtors' within one week of invoice date. Obviously this area of uncertainty is lessened considerably, as is the average time allowed for the revolving of working capital.

4.13   Factoring and the larger firm

The factor can therefore be instrumental in assisting the growing company to avoid management, financial, and prediction constraints that bar the way to the most efficient allocation of its resources, including management. This allows extension along the company's lowest possible cost curve. Generally factors find that their services are employed throughout the range of sales up to £5 million per annum after which the individual firm may be large enough to employ, in its own right, 'indivisible' resources used by the factor, and to bypass some of the constraints detailed above.

The figure of £5 million per annum is a very rough generalization as much depends upon the particular industry involved, and the functions undertaken by the individual company. Moreover, the factor may develop such a degree of specialization in certain areas that his services will be used by much larger companies who are unable to carry out equivalent functions with the same efficiency.

A particular example of this is to be found in the area of protection against bad debts. Here the factor can establish an unique knowledge of certain industries because it is factoring many clients in that industry and therefore has a constant knowledge of the paying habits of a large cross-section of customers. Examples are found within the portfolio of Walter E. Heller and Company. This factoring organization based in Chicago played a major part in factoring the developing synthetic fibre carpet industry in America, generating credit knowledge and operational procedures concerning that industry to a unique extent. As a result its services are now used by carpet manufacturers whose size would suggest that a factor's services would not be required. At the end of 1973 its largest client among the tufted carpet manufacturers was factoring sales at an annual rate approaching $145 million. This client started factoring in 1954 with factored sales approaching an annual rate of $20 million, and throughout the period found it beneficial to rely on the factor's expert knowledge of the industry rather than develop its own credit control department. Two other carpet manufacturing clients in the portfolio of Walter E. Heller and Company were, at the end of 1973, factoring sales at annual rates of $42 million and $26 million. The first client started factoring in 1968 with an annual sales rate of less than $1 million, and the second in 1966 with an annual sales rate of $600,000.

All three cases show first the ability of the factor to assist rapid growth and second that there will be situations, particularly where expansion is envisaged, where the normal criteria of cost comparison and effectiveness will not be sufficient to evaluate the factor's services. Unique credit knowledge allowing the avoidance of losses and the protection of working capital, while permitting speedy deliveries to creditworthy customers, may be purchased by the largest companies on the basis of sound commercial decisions.

4.2   COMPARISON WITH SOURCES OF SHORT-TERM FINANCE

The financial effect of a factoring facility, where the client receives payment against debts purchased prior to their settlement date, is concentrated upon the use of working capital. It operates to reduce the debtor item and is identical to debtors paying on cash or very short credit terms. Debtors are reduced, and short-term assets and liabilities re-arranged. Insofar as factoring is not a lending operation it is difficult to compare it exactly with lending facilities. However, the alternatives open to the finance manager in attempting to increase the utilization of working capital may be limited. Factoring facilities, for a variety of reasons, may not be available, and debtors may not be willing to pay on shorter terms even if cash discounts are offered which may be very expensive for the supplier.

In such circumstances the supplier may investigate sources of loan finance, predicated upon current assets, to enable expansion to continue. It is appropriate to compare factoring with these facilities so that the true relationship can be established. Essentially the main alternatives are bank overdraft, invoice discounting, sometimes styled 'confidential invoice factoring' or 'confidential invoice discounting', and undisclosed non-recourse finance.

4.21   Bank overdraft

For the majority of companies for whom factoring could be appropriate the bank overdraft, usually provided by the joint stock banks, is the most important source of short-term finance. Indeed the importance of this facility is such as totally to outweigh the present financial effect of factoring. The Report of the Committee of Inquiry on Small Firms, produced in November 1971, stated that 'External finance is synonymous for most small businessmen with bank overdraft'.* This statement is still substantially true today although knowledge of alternative facilities is now disseminated on a wider basis.

* *The Report of the Committee of Inquiry on Small Firms* (H.M.S.O. 1971), p. 160.

ADVANTAGES OF THE OVERDRAFT

As a financial facility the bank overdraft has many advantages. It is cheaper than other forms of short-term finance, interest being charged on the actual funds extended and related to bank base rate, with some spread to allow for the risk being undertaken in extending funds; it is flexible, as it can be used up to any agreed limit without any minimum value being stipulated, and repayment can be made at any time; it can be predicated upon specific security, very often in the form of a floating charge over all the assets of the business, or may be granted without security if the bank has a high opinion of management, assets, and profitability. A debenture on book debts alone is very unusual as the lender is not well-placed to compare the value of the constantly-changing security with the loan extended to the client.

While the bank overdraft is used on a semi-permanent basis by some companies, opinion has hardened that it exists essentially to assist working capital requirements, and that longer-term needs should be met by longer-term facilities. Intermittent utilization or complete repayment by an agreed date within a year of extending the overdraft is often required.

EXAMPLE OF EFFECTS OF AN OVERDRAFT

An example showing the effects of a bank overdraft, compared with an 'old line' factoring facility, is detailed in Table 4.2. The opening position (a) shows the situation of a small company with a barely satisfactory ratio of current assets to current liabilities of 1·25:1. To provide more flexibility in paying creditors in order to obtain cash discounts, and to allow purchase of stock at advantageous times, the company can obtain a factoring facility providing for payments of 80 per cent of the value of outstanding trade debts sold or can obtain an equivalent bank overdraft.

The immediate effects of these alternatives are shown in positions (b) and (d). The factoring facility has not increased current assets, but simply re-arranged them by replacing debtors with cash. Unlike the bank overdraft situation, current liabilities have not been increased as the factor is a debtor, to the extent of the reserve of £3,000, and not a creditor as is the bank, for £12,000. The use of the factoring facility has left the ratio of current assets to current liabilities unchanged, while the use of the bank overdraft has changed this ratio unfavourably.

In practice the cash asset would be put to immediate use, and positions (c) and (e) show the situation after the company has paid overdue creditors of £10,000 and increased stock by £1,000. Effecting these changes by a factoring facility has increased the ratio of current assets to current liabilities to 1·5:1, while the use of a bank overdraft has not quite repaired the original

Table 4.2

COMPARATIVE EFFECTS OF A FACTORING FACILITY AND A BANK OVERDRAFT

(a) Initial position

	£			£
Issued Capital and Reserves	15,000	Fixed Assets		10,000
Creditors	20,000	Stock	10,000	
		Debtors	15,000	
				25,000
	£35,000			**£35,000**

(b) Factoring facility with 80% payment against debts

	£			£
Issued Capital and Reserves	15,000	Fixed Assets		10,000
Creditors	20,000	Stock	10,000	
		Balance due from Factor	3,000	
		Cash	12,000	
				25,000
	£35,000			**£35,000**

(c) Use of cash asset to reduce creditors £10,000, increase stock £1,000, after (b)

	£			£
Issued Capital and Reserves	15,000	Fixed Assets		10,000
Creditors	10,000	Stock	11,000	
		Balance due from Factor	3,000	
		Cash	1,000	
				15,000
	£25,000			**£25,000**

(d) Bank overdraft for £12,000

	£			£
Issued Capital and Reserves		15,000	Fixed Assets		10,000
Bank Overdraft	12,000		Stock	10,000	
Creditors	20,000		Debtors	15,000	
		32,000	Cash	12,000	
					37,000
		£47,000			**£47,000**

(e) Use of cash asset to reduce creditors £10,000, increase stock £1,000, after (d)

	£			£
Issued Capital and Reserves		15,000	Fixed Assets		10,000
Bank Overdraft	12,000		Stock	11,000	
Creditors	10,000		Debtors	15,000	
		22,000	Cash	1,000	
					27,000
		£37,000			**£37,000**

Ratio of current assets to current liabilities in above positions:
(a) 1·25 : 1   (b) 1·25 : 1   (c) 1·5 : 1   (d) 1·16 : 1
(e) 1·23 : 1

deterioration in the ratio of current assets to current liabilities. Use of the factoring facility has had a positive effect on the ratio of current assets to current liabilities, and in this respect has strengthened the balance sheet and credit standing of the user.

The above example is not meant to be definitive as much depends upon the use of the current asset of cash. Nevertheless, it does show that the factoring facility can have a positive effect on the balance sheet of the user.

4.22   Confidential invoice discounting

While confidential invoice discounting is often stated to be an alternative to factoring, it is designed to satisfy different needs. Generally invoices are transferred to the lender on a with recourse basis and the borrower, or client, will carry out all ledgering and collection work as existed prior to the discounting arrangement. Moreover the client may be able to select trade debts that should be offered under the facility to the invoice discounting house. Because the invoice discounter maintains a surveillance of the major credit exposures and, at intervals, carries out investigations of debtor administration by the client, it is often possible to generate a larger loan against outstanding trade debts than would be the case if there were a bank overdraft arrangement. Occasionally payments from customers will be controlled in such a way that the invoice discounter can ensure that funds are not improperly directed.

The financial aspect of the invoice discount facility is paramount and, in certain cases, can be more appropriate than factoring if the factoring service is not required. However, in general the client has to maintain additional records to fulfil the requirements of the invoice discounter and must meet higher standards regarding size and profitability. The user also has to face the prospect of having to repay the invoice discounter when trade debts become overdue. In some cases, bills of exchange may be drawn against such trade debts and presented on due date whether or not such debts have been paid by the customer to the client.

In essence, therefore, the client is obtaining additional borrowing facilities while, on the contrary, under a factoring arrangement he is simply making more efficient use of his own working capital. Perhaps a better comparison is to liken the invoice discounting facility to an extension of a bank overdraft secured on the book debt item in a specialized manner, allowing for additional funds to be made available; these are usually at a higher rate than that charged by the bank for bank overdraft facilities.

4.23   Undisclosed non-recourse finance

A facility nearer in effect to factoring is the undisclosed non-recourse finance facility, under which the client will sell goods to the finance house and thereafter sell those goods to specified customers acting as agent of the finance house, unknown to the customer. The client is paid for the goods by the finance house upon delivery to the customer, at a percentage of the final sales price. The risk of customer bad debt is taken by the finance house, who is paid by the client collecting and remitting the relevant funds as his agent. Again the ledgering and collection services are absent, but effectively 100 per cent credit protection has been extended on those customers selected by the finance house for this facility. A loan position has not occurred since the client has effectively transferred a credit into a cash sale.

While of use in many situations, this facility is not as widespread as factoring or invoice discounting, and is generally applied to much larger and stronger companies who are able to offer large trade debt transactions covering sales to a few well-rated customers. Again, the client will incur more rather than less administrative work in complying with the requirements of the finance house. He cannot require the major services offered by the factoring operation which would apply to the total sales ledger.

APPENDIX TO CHAPTER 4

Effect of factoring upon output, costs, and prices

EFFECT OF FACTORING UPON A FIRM

Figure 4.1 shows a situation where the efficient firm wishing to expand along its marginal cost curve to an output of OM in order to meet the

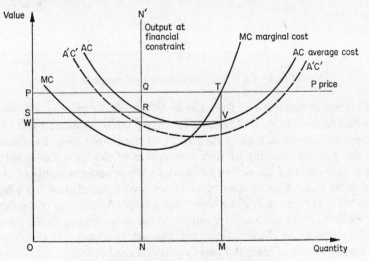

FIGURE 4.1. Effect of factoring on a firm.

demand for the product at the price OP can be prevented from doing this because of lack of velocity of working capital. It is restricted to production of ON earning profits of PQRS (the difference between average cost OS and average price OP applied to production ON) instead of PTVW at output OM. The financial constraint placed upon output, reduction of costs, and increased profits can be removed by factoring, as working capital is returned to the firm almost immediately after the trade debt has been created. Moreover, by applying the principle of specialization of resources to the functions carried out by the factor, a more efficient firm can result, giving rise to an average cost curve A'C' as against an original cost curve AC.

EFFECT OF FACTORING UPON AN INDUSTRY

Figure 4.2 shows these effects translated into an industry supply curve which shifts from S1 to S2, causing resources to be used more efficiently

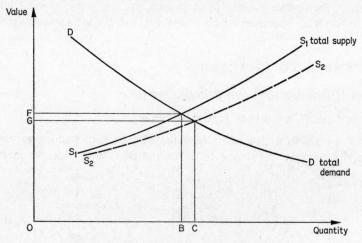

FIGURE 4.2.   Effect of factoring on an industry.

and output to be increased from OB to OC, while the price of the product is reduced from OF to OG. The flatter supply curve is caused by the more efficient producers increasing their share of the output from the industry, and the general lowering of such cost curves of the individual producer. The supply curve of the industry as a whole is composed not only of individual firms expanding to meet higher price levels, but also of less efficient firms being brought in at those higher price levels. Application of the factoring facility allows the industry supply curve to assume a flatter upward slope as the more efficient firms are allowed to expand to their proper economic size (until marginal costs equal marginal revenue), thus delaying the entry of the less efficient firm.

Part Two: The Management of Working Capital

5 Working Capital and Solvency

5.1 BASIC DEFINITIONS AND COMPONENT PARTS OF WORKING CAPITAL

5.11 Basic definitions

Working capital refers to a firm's investment in short-term or current assets—cash, trade debts, and stocks. Working capital is that part of capital which is circulating from cash to stock to trade debts and back into cash again within a relatively short time. This is normally assumed to be less than one year, but is more accurately defined as the operating cycle of the firm, which might be as short as seven days or as long as eighteen months.

Net working capital is the difference between current assets and current liabilities, between the short-term assets of the firm and its short-term obligations. The term working capital is sometimes used to refer to what has been defined above as net working capital. However, the term working capital used in this chapter without further qualification refers to cash, trade debts, and stocks.

5.12 Component parts of working capital

CASH

The finance manager must make certain that the investment in cash is efficiently used. He will wish to ensure that cash inflows are speeded up whilst disbursements are slowed down, thereby keeping the cost of financing the stock of cash to a minimum.

Efficient financial management, however, stresses maximization of profit functions which involves cost functions. If as a result of delaying cash payments the firm loses a two and a half per cent discount on the seventh day past settlement date and subsequently pays the net amount on the thirtieth day, the cost to the firm is 39·7 per cent, calculated as follows:

$$\text{Discount rate} \times \frac{\text{Days in year}}{\text{Settlement period} - \text{discount period}}$$

TRADE DEBTS

Trade debts represent open account credit extended by the firm. Through variations in the length of the credit period, cash discount terms, the credit line granted, and the criteria for selecting customers, the level of trade debts outstanding and the risk of ultimate uncollectability may be altered. For example, increases in the length of the credit period may increase demand for the firm's product but it may also increase the likelihood of non-collection. Similarly, a decision to incur additional expenses by commencing legal action at an earlier point in the collection cycle should be compensated for by a shortening of the credit period and a reduction in the number of bad debts sustained.

STOCK

Stock can usually be divided into three separate sub-sections—raw materials, work in progress, and finished goods.

The levels of raw materials are influenced by anticipated production, seasonal nature of production, reliability of sources of supply, and the productive efficiency of the firm itself. Work in progress is strongly influenced by the length of the production process, while the level of finished goods stock is mainly a matter of co-ordination between the production and sales function. It is irrelevant from the financing point of view whether the goods are held as finished stock or as receivables, although it is normally preferable to take the latter course since the potential profits usually outweigh the additional collection risks.

5.2 SOLVENCY RATIOS

The short-term suppliers of capital, while interested in the profitability of the firm, are primarily concerned with a firm's short-term liquid balances; by contrast, long-term suppliers of capital are primarily interested in profitability. Liquidity means cash and cash availability, and it is from current operations and previous accumulations that cash is available to satisfy the claims of both short and long-term suppliers of capital.

5.21 Short-term liquidity ratios

Analysis of a firm's short-term liquidity position is usually centred on the series of ratios set out in Table 5.1. These are derived from information

Table 5.1

SHORT-TERM LIQUIDITY RATIOS

CURRENT	$\dfrac{\text{Current Assets}}{\text{Current Liabilities}}$
QUICK OR ACID	$\dfrac{\text{Current Assets} - \text{Stock}}{\text{Current Liabilities}}$
STOCK TURNOVER	$\dfrac{\text{Cost of Goods Sold}}{\text{Average Stock}}$
DEBTORS TURNOVER	$\dfrac{\text{Credit Sales}}{\text{Average Debtors}}$

which can be obtained from the firm's published balance sheet and profit and loss account. The purpose of short-term ratio analysis is to formulate an opinion of the firm's capacity to meet its short-term obligations out of its short-term resources, that is, to estimate the risk of supplying short-term capital to the firm.

THE CURRENT RATIO

The first ratio typically used in short-term analysis is the current ratio, which compares the firm's total current assets to its total current liabilities. Included in the current assets are cash and all assets that are expected to be converted into cash in one year within the normal course of operations. Current liabilities consist of the claims of short-term creditors which have to be settled within the course of one year, and include current maturities of long-term indebtedness and amounts owed to trade creditors.

It is difficult to judge what is a satisfactory current ratio for any firm, but for most manufacturing firms a ratio of current assets to current liabilities of 2:1 has traditionally been considered adequate. It is important to remember, however, that this ratio, like all those that rely only on balance sheet information, shows the position at a given moment in time which may be a significant point in reviewing a firm subject to seasonal fluctuations in activity. It does not comment on the time period in which the short-term creditors' claims must be met or the estimated time period for converting cash to stocks to trade debts to cash again. There is no certainty that the current assets can be converted into cash at their stated values on the balance sheet, while in Table 4.2 we saw that it is a relatively easy process to manipulate the current ratio by reorganizing a firm's net working capital position.

THE QUICK RATIO OR ACID TEST

The quick ratio is developed from the current ratio and reflects the doubts surrounding the probable valuation of the least liquid asset of all current assets, stock, in the event of the firm's liquidation. Stock is therefore excluded from the numerator, and the resulting ratio will give a measure of the firm's ability to pay off short-term obligations without relying upon the sale of stock. The quick ratio does not replace the current ratio but supplements it, the two being used together to give a more balanced view of the firm's ability to meet its short-term creditors.

A variation of this ratio is the number of days needed to generate sufficient funds from operations to cover the difference between current liabilities and quick assets. This measure should be important to the suppliers of short-term capital when the quick ratio falls below its traditionally accepted standard of 1:1. The formula to calculate the number of days is as follows:

$$\frac{\text{Current Liabilities} - \text{Quick Assets}}{\text{Funds from Operations}} \times 365 \text{ days}$$

Funds from operations in any period are calculated by adding to net profit all non-cash expenses such as depreciation. For the purpose of this calculation all capital cash inflows and disbursements are ignored.

The following example illustrates this, the relevant information being set out in Table 5.2.

Table 5.2

NUMBER OF DAYS REQUIRED TO COVER DIFFERENCE BETWEEN CURRENT LIABILITIES AND QUICK ASSETS

BALANCE SHEET XYZ LTD

Capital		£15,000	Fixed Assets		£10,000
Current Liabilities			Current Assets		
Trade Creditors	24,000		Stock	7,000	
Bank Overdraft	1,000	25,000	Debtors	23,000	30,000
		£40,000			£40,000

PROFIT AND LOSS STATEMENT
XYZ LTD

Net Profit, after Depreciation	£8,000
Add back: Depreciation	2,000
Funds Generated from Operations	£10,000

Number of days required to cover differences between current liabilities and quick assets

$$= \frac{£(25,000 - 23,000)}{£10,000} \times 365 \text{ days}$$

$$= \frac{£ \ 2,000}{£10,000} \times 365 \text{ days}$$

$$= 73 \text{ days}$$

STOCK TURNOVER RATIO

This ratio relates the cost of goods sold during a period to the average stock carried, and is calculated in the following manner:

$$\frac{\text{Cost of Goods Sold}}{(\text{Beginning Stock} + \text{Ending Stock}) \ / \ 2}$$

It establishes the number of times that stock is converted into sales over a period, and while there is no generally accepted standard for this ratio, comparison with other firms in the industry may provide an indication as to whether the firm's investment in stock is reasonable.

Whereas the current and quick ratios are concerned with measuring the extent to which short-term obligations are covered by short-term assets and use static information taken from the balance sheet only, the stock turnover ratio and the debtors turnover ratio considered below attempt to measure the rate of cash flow through the firm. The former indicates the number of times that inventory is converted into sales giving rise to trade debts; these trade debts are turned into cash after a further delay, the extent of which is quantified by the second ratio.

DEBTORS TURNOVER RATIO

The debtors turnover ratio relates a firm's credit sales to its trade debtors and indicates the number of times that sales are turned into cash during a period. This measure can then be extended to show the number of days that on average a firm has to wait before converting trade debts into cash. As with the stock turnover ratio, there are no special standards by which to judge the correctness of any debtors' turnover ratio, but comparison with other firms in the industry will often indicate the soundness or otherwise of an individual firm's credit and collection procedures.

CONVERSION PERIOD FOR STOCKS

The stock and debtors turnover ratios can be combined to indicate the length of time needed to convert stock into cash, calculated in the following manner:

$$\frac{365}{\text{No. of times stock turns over}} = \text{Days to sell stock}$$

$$\frac{365}{\text{No. of times debtors turn over}} = \text{Days to collect debts}$$

$$\overline{\text{Conversion period for stock in days}}$$

The firm must have access to sufficient capital resources to finance the conversion period for stock less the period of credit granted by the stock supplier. Where the firm does not have the necessary capital resources to keep within the normal credit period stipulated by suppliers, a position of overtrading has been reached.

Before considering this phenomenon in greater detail (*see* 5.3), long-term liquidity ratios are considered briefly.

5.22 Long-term liquidity ratios

It is not the purpose of this book to consider in detail the long-term capital structures of firms. Short-term liquidity, however, cannot be viewed as being completely in a vacuum and unaffected by long-term liquidity criteria. It is therefore necessary to indicate the major requirements of the suppliers of long-term funds so that the subject matter of this chapter may be seen in perspective.

Whereas the suppliers of short-term capital concentrate upon a set of ratios dependent upon information in the balance sheet, the suppliers of long-term capital will concentrate upon a set of ratios dependent upon the profit and loss account for an indication of the long-term liquidity of the firm. The object of these ratios is to measure the extent to which the various financial claims on the earnings of the firm are covered out of current results, and they reflect the importance of profits to the supplier of long-term capital.

Profitability is important because of the presumption that payment of interest or dividends and repayment of principal can only be derived from the profit stream of the firm. Short-term suppliers of capital will consider profitability to be of secondary importance, and will concentrate their attention on ensuring that the firm has sufficient cash or near cash stocks to meet short-term obligations, as they fall due for payment.

In addition to concentrating upon an analysis of the firm's profitability, the suppliers of long-term capital will wish to measure the proportion of capital supplied by the owners. It is fundamental to financing mix problems that under normal circumstances the owners of the firm should assume the greater proportion of the risks and rewards from carrying on the business. The correct relationship between the amount of funds supplied by the owners and by their creditors is a matter of judgment in each case. Firms with relatively low business risks will obviously be able to raise a greater proportion of their total capital requirements from creditors than those who show widely fluctuating earnings from year to year, thereby indicating high business risk.

A summary of the ratios that suppliers of long-term capital have developed is set out in Table 5.3.

Table 5.3

LONG-TERM MEASURES OF SOLVENCY

(a) *Profitability Ratios*

TURNOVER
$$\frac{\text{Sales}}{\text{Total Assets}}$$

GROSS PROFIT
$$\frac{\text{Gross Profit}}{\text{Sales}}$$

RETURN ON CAPITAL
$$\frac{\text{Net Profit after Tax}}{\text{Capital}}$$

(b) *Long-term Liquidity Ratios*

BORROWINGS – CAPITAL
$$\frac{\text{Borrowings}}{\text{Shareholders' Funds}}$$

INTEREST COVERAGE
$$\frac{\text{Profit before Tax and Interest}}{\text{Interest Expense}}$$

5.3 OVERTRADING

5.31 Definition of overtrading

In Chapter 2 it was indicated that a firm's working capital requirement tends to be a function of sales, that is, higher levels of stock, trade debts, and cash have to be carried to support any increases in turnover. In addition, working capital was analyzed as to whether it was of a permanent or fluctuating nature. Permanent working capital is the amount of current assets required by the business to cover normal production; fluctuating working capital is the addition to permanent working capital required to cover seasonal variations in production, above that normally undertaken.

It was suggested in Chapter 2 that permanent working capital should be financed from the permanent sources of capital available to the firm, while the fluctuations above this base should be financed by variable short-term sources according to need. While no discussion as to the optimum level of working capital was undertaken, it was implicitly assumed that the firm was always able to achieve equilibrium between the competing pressures of carrying sufficient stocks of current assets to support the level of sales, and obtaining sufficient capital to finance them.

Included in the sources of finance is the trade credit which is spontaneously created by suppliers providing goods on open credit terms. However, unless the firm's stock conversion time discussed above (*see* page 52) is the same or shorter than the credit period granted by suppliers, the firm will need access to additional liquid funds to meet the demands of its creditors. A firm can obviously delay payments to its suppliers for a certain length of time, but if this becomes a habit the credit standing of the firm will suffer, which will eventually lead to a stoppage of supplies.

Overtrading can therefore be defined as occurring once a firm is forced, through lack of adequate liquid resources, to extend the period of credit taken from its suppliers beyond the terms agreed, which can be explicitly defined or implied from allowed payment patterns. Although a narrow definition, it does serve to highlight the combination of circumstances that can lead to overtrading.

5.32 Effects of overtrading

The most common feature of a firm overtrading is too narrow a capital base from which a rapid expansion of sales takes place. While the firm remains at normal growth rates, the owners can exercise tight control over the collection of trade debts, any increases in liquidity being met by retained profits. If, however, changes in demand occur and the firm's product becomes sought after, the owners will often try to meet the increased market without arranging additional capital resources, either of a short or long-term nature.

During the initial expansion period, liquidity is unlikely to become strained, because demand for the product is such that the firm can stipulate cash on delivery or seven days payment, while raw materials are purchased on normal trade credit terms. However, as the company expands its sales, administration problems in policing the trade debts occur as the number of debtors increase and the collection period starts to lengthen, with a detrimental effect on the firm's cash flow. Payment to suppliers has to be delayed, which eventually results in goods being withheld, thereby affecting the production process as stocks of certain items become depleted. The stock conversion period is thus lengthened and the company's cash problems are further intensified. The options facing the company at this point are liquidation or a substantial injection of funds to enable the trade creditors to resume supplies once their old balances have been extinguished.

A management which is prepared to permit a decrease in the firm's liquidity, from the optimal point at which the demands of creditors can always be met at due date, incurs other expenses which are difficult to cost in the short term—lost cash discount, stock out, and poor credit ratings. The cumulative effect of these expenses may be to decrease profitability to the point of an uneconomic return on capital employed, which would place the continued existence of the firm in jeopardy.

6 Cash Management

6.1 STOCKS AND FLOWS OF CASH

From the outset it is important to emphasize the distinction between stocks and flows of cash. The balance in the bank account measures the stock of cash. A flow may be an inflow or outflow; if the inflow exceeds the outflow the stock will rise and if the outflow exceeds the inflow the stock will fall. The stock is measured at a point in time such as that reflected on a balance sheet, whereas a flow is measured as a rate per period of time, such as income per year. Both stocks and flows are of interest to the financial manager, because the amount of cash and the rate at which it flows through the company as a result of operations primarily determines the ability of the firm to pay creditors, to take on new capital projects, and to pay dividends.

6.11 Need for a stock of cash

The company's need for a stock of cash centres on the transactionary, precautionary, and speculative motives for holding cash. If the cash inflows equalled cash outflows at all times, there would be no necessity to hold cash for transaction purposes; the two, however, are rarely synchronized. Even if they were expected to be synchronized, the financial manager would still face a degree of uncertainty as to the exact time of the inflows and outflows, and it is because of this uncertainty that the financial manager will hold cash for precautionary purposes.

The speculative motive for holding cash is to take advantage of any profit-making opportunities that may arise. For example, the financial manager may hold cash in anticipation of a decline in the price of certain raw materials, when the supplier will require cash with order. However, since the financial manager's principal function is not speculation but to assist in the production process, we shall concentrate on the transactionary and precautionary motives for holding cash.

Planning for a stock of cash at a point in time for transactionary and precautionary purposes involves a study of cash inflows and outflows from operations. A financial manager might well plot his cash flow for a typical month, as shown in Figure 6.1. Curve PO represents cash outlays, points A, B, C, and D indicating weekly wage payments, and point X the payment of creditors. Curve PI shows cash inflows, the majority of debts being paid in the second week of the month. For the first part of the month, until PI intersects PO at point R, cash outflows exceed cash inflows, and the stock of cash at the beginning of the month must be sufficient to cover the

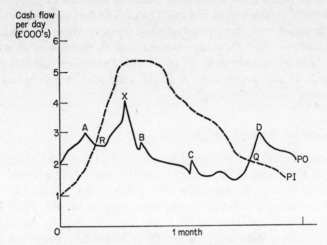

FIGURE 6.1.   Daily cash flows in a month.

net outflow. From point R to point Q the company's daily inflow exceeds the daily outflow, and the stock of cash held increases. Stock will be depleted, however, once point Q is past as, in the last period of the month, cash outflows exceed inflows again.

In this example, it is obvious that for precautionary purposes a stock of cash should be available during the opening and closing periods of the month. As an aid to establishing the size of the cash balance required for precautionary motives, the financial manager should consider constructing a number of graphs representing past monthly cash flows. These will give an indication of expected movement in a month's cash flow, provided that there is no underlying change in the company's pattern of trading.

The size of the precautionary balance would obviously be reduced if funds were readily available from other sources such as banks and factors. A good long-term relationship with such financial institutions, particularly in those instances where a company's trade is highly seasonal, would result in much smaller precautionary reserves being held than would otherwise be the case.

6.2 THE CASH BUDGET

In financial planning, the flow of cash is as important as the stock of cash, a fact recognized by the majority of companies which utilize some form of cash budgeting. A cash budget provides detailed short-term cash planning, predicting all inflows and outflows of cash and expected excesses or shortages of cash at certain points in time. The cash budget is an important tool for the financial manager in maintaining liquidity, since it indicates the likely occasions when the cash on hand will be insufficient to meet the company's needs. It is normally constructed on the basis of monthly periods, as it is not usually practical to highlight variations in a company's cash requirements over a shorter period.

6.21 Preparing the cash budget

To prepare the cash budget, it will be necessary to know the expected level of sales in the period under review, the company's selling terms, and its past experience in collecting trade debts, before cash receipts can be estimated. For example, if January sales are estimated to be £12,000 and the firm sells on ordinary terms of net thirty days (all invoices are due thirty days after the invoice date), it would examine its previous collection experience to determine that 50 per cent (£6,000) of January sales are collected in February, 40 per cent (£4,800) are collected in March, and the balance in April.

From forecasts of sales and actual stock levels of raw materials, work in progress, and finished goods, the financial manager is able to plan production which will enable him to determine the amount of cash to be expended on materials and labour. Bought-in goods have to be ordered early enough to ensure delivery by the time the material is needed for production and delivery dates, when taken in conjunction with purchase credit terms, can be used to determine a payment schedule for trade creditors.

6.22 Example of a cash budget and worksheet

The various data can be organized into a cash budget and worksheet such as the one illustrated in Table 6.1. In this example, it is assumed that purchases of materials and supplies are ordered and delivered a month ahead of production, and paid for at the beginning of the month following production. It is also assumed that 10 per cent of sales are collected in the first month following sale, 50 per cent in the second month, and the balance in the third month. The financial manager estimates that at the beginning of

Table 6.1   CASH BUDGET AND WORKSHEET ABC LTD.

WORKSHEET

	October	November	December	January	February	March	April	May	June	July
Sales	£20,000	£10,000	£10,000	£15,000	£30,000	£40,000	£40,000	£20,000	£10,000	£10,000
Collections										
First month (10%)		£2,000	£1,000	£1,000	£1,500	£3,000	£4,000	£4,000	£2,000	£1,000
Second month (50%)			10,000	5,000	5,000	7,500	15,000	20,000	20,000	10,000
Third month (40%)				8,000	4,000	4,000	6,000	12,000	16,000	16,000
TOTAL		£2,000	£11,000	£14,000	£10,500	£14,500	£25,000	£36,000	£38,000	£27,000
Purchase (60% of next month's sales)		£6,000	£9,000	£18,000	£24,000	£24,000	£12,000	£6,000	£6,000	

CASH BUDGET

	January	February	March	April	May	June
Receipts	£14,000	£10,500	£14,500	£25,000	£36,000	£38,000
Payments						
Purchases	6,000	9,000	18,000	24,000	24,000	12,000
Wages	1,000	1,500	1,750	1,750	1,250	1,000
Other expenses	300	400	400	400	350	300
Capital purchases	5,800	—	—	—	—	—
Taxes	1,500	—	—	—	—	—
Rent	3,000	—	—	3,000	—	—
TOTAL PAYMENTS	£17,600	£10,900	£20,150	£29,150	£25,600	£13,300
Net cash inflow/(outflow) in month	(£ 3,600)	(£ 400)	(£ 5,650)	(£ 4,150)	£10,400	£24,700
Opening cash balance	3,600	—	(400)	(6,050)	(10,200)	200
Closing cash balance/(deficit)	—	(400)	(6,050)	(10,200)	200	24,900
Required cash balance	3,000	3,000	3,000	3,000	3,000	3,000
Cash in excess/(below) required balance	(£ 3,000)	(£ 3,400)	(£ 9,050)	(£13,200)	(£ 2,800)	£21,900

any month a cash balance of £3,000 is acquired to cover both the transactionary and precautionary motives for holding cash; the initial cash balance on January 1 is £3,600.

Basing decisions upon these estimates, the financial manager should plan to borrow progressively by month up to a maximum figure of £13,200 in April, and to repay the amount in June. Knowing when cash deficiencies will arise enables the financial manager to seek out additional sources of capital well in advance of actual need. By contrast, the financial manager, in viewing the extra large predicted cash balances in June, should consider alternative uses for these funds in order to maximize profits. If the cash is not needed to meet dividends or capital expenditures immediately, consideration should be given to investing the funds in short-term securities or, perhaps, to repaying outstanding liabilities. Funds could be used, for example, to repay a short-term loan and, when needed later in the year, a loan could be recreated. Similarly, cash discounts for prompt payment previously foregone can now be taken.

The financial manager may obviously project his cash planning beyond the six-month period used in the example. Six months is a common period of time in that the more distant projects become the greater the uncertainty that surrounds them. In spite of this limitation, the foregoing discussion indicates that the cash budget is extremely useful as a planning tool, provided that management always bears in mind that the budget is based on estimates and that the further a period is from the present the more uncertain are the estimates.

6.3   CASH AS A LIMITING FACTOR

6.31   The use of trade credit

Trade on open credit terms is one of the most important short-term sources of capital available to companies in the United Kingdom. Although trade credit is not directly a source of cash, the fact that payment is deferred permits a company to secure the benefits of goods and services immediately, without incurring costs which could arise from depleting its stock of cash or securing funds elsewhere. A company that does not satisfy the strict criteria for funding from the financial institutions will probably receive trade credit from suppliers, because through previous dealings its credit standing will have been established.

Trade credit is a customary part of everyday business life and tends to be both an informal and spontaneous source of finance. It is informal and spontaneous in that it arises in the ordinary course of business. For example, if a company makes average purchases of £500 a day on thirty day terms, it will on average owe £15,000 to its suppliers at any point in time, provided that the selling terms are adhered to. Should sales double, purchases will also double and provided that suppliers have had no reason to doubt the company's credit standing in the past, then it is highly probable that the additional purchases will be made available on a credit basis. Suppliers will thus be owed £30,000 on average at any one time, and the company will have spontaneously generated an additional £15,000 of finance.

6.32 The restricting of trade credit

Trade credit, although of great importance in the financial structure of many companies, is a privilege extended by the supplier and not a right to be relied upon by the customer. A financial manager's decision to delay payment of suppliers' accounts should not be based upon the costs of discount foregone or the explicit interest costs avoided by not increasing the company's borrowings, but upon qualitative factors such as the effect of a loss of confidence in the company by its suppliers. It is possible, for example, that while such action would be successful in alleviating a short-term cash flow problem, the long-term result could be to reduce the financing alternatives available to the company in subsequent periods.

The company must devise a financial policy which not only recognizes the varying claims of the suppliers of capital on the company, but allows settlement of those claims on due date. While lack of cash will result in discount for prompt settlement being lost and may prevent the company from taking advantage of favourable business opportunities that may arise from time to time, these disadvantages pale into insignificance when compared with the irreparable damage that may occur if the suppliers of finance have reason to doubt the company's payment capabilities.

The financial manager will therefore often find himself having to restrict the amount of trade credit which is incurred, and thus the level of sales that can be achieved. He must do this in order to ensure that the company's liquidity is preserved at a level which will give confidence to all suppliers of capital, and particularly those of a short-term nature, that the company will meet its obligations on due date.

7 Credit Control

7.1 THE NEED FOR A CREDIT CONTROL POLICY

Industrial and commercial trade credit is the most important form of financial assistance given throughout the economy of the United Kingdom, far exceeding bank credit extended to industry, or hire purchase and leasing facilities. It is the cheapest form of credit to receive, being free of interest— and the dearest form of finance to extend.

7.11 The cost of trade credit

In many cases a contract of sale between industrial and commercial companies will carry an explicit, or implicit, condition that the time of payment by the buyer should be later than the time of supply of goods or rendering of services by the seller, giving rise to the extending of trade credit. Thus, a car component manufacturer producing engine parts on payment terms of net settlement at end of month following month of invoice is extending, on average, forty-five days credit to his customers. If his money cost is, for example, 10 per cent per annum this is equivalent to an increase in cost of $1\frac{1}{4}$ per cent, so that £10,000 of supplies incurs an additional cost of £125. If his customers take a further month before paying this adds a further £83·33 to the cost, making a total in excess of £200. The more protracted the payment the higher the cost to the producer, the finite cost only being established if the debt is paid or becomes a bad debt.

7.12 Importance of a flexible policy

In addition to the objective of minimizing the cost of credit extended to customers, the producer must aim at ensuring that the cash forecasts relating to the flow of funds in and out of his business allow for the business to be conducted without strain, and that such cash forecasts are upheld. Not only does trade credit extended beyond what is necessary cost more and reduce profitability, but working capital may also be insufficient for the business to continue at present levels. Credit taken from trade creditors and other sources may be stretched by the producer with disastrous results. This can lead to the opposite result to that intended when creditors restrict credit to the producer, creating a vicious spiral that can end in disaster.

The necessity to collect trade debts as quickly as possible should be, therefore, high on the list of priorities, yet this must be married to the objective of avoiding the loss of any creditworthy customers due to undue collection pressure. In this situation a clearly-defined credit control policy is essential, to provide an operating framework within which credit control procedures can be applied to constantly-changing circumstances. It is no use setting down the basis upon which credit is to be extended to customers, if the actual decision is not constantly reviewed in the light of changed situations.

The continued granting of credit can be compared with the stretching of a piece of elastic. Just as the credit manager compares the amount of credit given (both as to value and period) against known facts concerning the customer, so one can compare the stress on the elastic (as to degree and time) created by stretching it with the strength of the elastic. Each time pressure is applied such pressure will vary and may well cause a reduction in the strength of the elastic. At some point one may decide that stress borne hitherto will not be withstood because of wear and tear to date. The underlying data, namely the strength of the elastic, has changed.

Similarly the credit manager must assess the credit to be given, from time to time, against the strength of the customer, and this will also vary throughout time. The granting of a credit limit with reference to information available in January 1960 and the ignoring of danger signals from late 1960 in terms of delayed payment, charges being taken over the customer's assets, and recording of County Court judgments against the customer, all culminating in liquidation and credit loss by the middle of 1961, is evidence of an ill-conceived credit control policy in need of serious overhaul, or one which is being ignored.

7.2 ESTABLISHING AN INTEGRATED CREDIT CONTROL POLICY

To establish a credit policy it is necessary to consider the credit control section and its powers in relation to the other departments of the company. This should be agreed with all department heads and confirmed in writing to avoid any doubt in future transactions. Credit control cannot operate in a vacuum as it directly affects the operations of sales, production, and finance departments, and its integration with these functions is essential.

Points that should be covered specifically are dealt with in the following section.

7.21   The power of the Credit Control Department

Even though the objective of the credit control department should be a positive one in attempting to authorize deliveries to customers, there will, nevertheless, be occasions when the credit manager will not wish to authorize such deliveries in direct opposition to the desires of the sales or marketing department. The power of the credit control department must therefore be clearly defined as to:

1. The levels up to which the department can establish credit lines for each customer. Also whether such limits must be authorized by the credit manager or can be delegated to subordinates. Finally the information necessary for establishing such limits. For example, a company selling to 1,000 customers with a total sales volume of more than £1 million per annum may decide that first orders up to £50 may be automatically authorized upon receipt of a satisfactory report from the sales representative. Above this figure bank and trade references, or credit register information may be required, and any lines above, say, £500 may require substantiating by reference to a credit agency report.

2. The powers of the department to refuse to authorize deliveries if a credit limit set by the credit manager (or delegated subordinate) would be exceeded by such deliveries. No point is served by establishing credit limits which are not adhered to by the company when the customer is calling for more deliveries.

3. The credit trading terms of the company and the degree of tolerance to be allowed for any discount terms that are detailed. The authority to vary selling terms should be clearly defined.

4. The general collection procedures within which the credit control policy must be executed. This will include the frequency of letters, the method of approach, and the period after which final collection methods, such as resort to legal action or debt collection agencies, must be undertaken. Within this general policy the credit manager should have the authority to vary collection procedures on individual customers, provided that there is justification for such a course of action. It is more than justified for a credit manager to make a personal and periodic visit to a major customer to reconcile any differences on sales and purchase ledgers, and collect a cheque for, say, £15,000. Not only may this save many hundreds of pounds annually in interest, but it may add to the goodwill existing between supplier and buyer, while containing the customer exposure.

5. Communication with other departments when a certain stage of collection has been reached. The order department and sales representative should be aware of a difficult collection situation, when the customer is

taking extended credit. Very often the refusal of further orders may stimulate the customer to make payments. Similarly senior management should be aware of impending bad debts or disputes preventing settlement of accounts.

7.22 Position of executive responsible for credit policy

This will depend upon the size and scope of the individual company. Too often the function of credit control may be only one of the responsibilities of a senior executive, so that decisions taken may be overridden by the conflicting requirements of the sales manager or director totally concerned with the sales function. In this situation, if the company is too small to employ a credit controller on a full-time basis, it is best to delegate the authority to a middle executive as a major function, ensuring that sufficient force is given to the views of the credit control department. A direct link between the credit control manager and the board (or managing director) must be established, possibly with the company secretary or chief accountant existing as a link.

7.3 SOURCES OF CREDIT INFORMATION

The problem facing the credit manager is generally raised by the nature of trading between his company and the customer. If the supplier is engaged in trades such as shipbuilding, heavy engineering, and property construction, the credit decision is often based upon the gathering of detailed information on the status of the buyer at the commencement of the contract, and in many cases upon the obtaining of credit insurance cover. Such information will be updated throughout the period of the contract. The sources of such information are discussed later, but these may be reinforced, in such contractual negotiations, by detailed information supplied by the buyer regarding his financial situation. Moreover, the buyer's standing could be such that detailed information may be a matter of public record, for example if the buyer is a public company.

In many cases the buyer may appear undoubted, but recent history shows this is not always the case. Of more importance, the credit decision may be subordinated to the weighing of the risk of loss through an uncompleted contract which may stretch well beyond the period of normal credit. The supplier that has half completed a specialized heavy-duty engine will incur heavy loss if the buyer ceases to exist, even if credit, as defined in this chapter, has not been granted. The terms of each contract will, in this method of trading, usually incorporate specific credit and contractual payments.

Alternatively, in many cases, the supplier may be dealing with the customer on a continuing basis, so that the credit manager will be faced with a stream of credit decisions (a continual stretching and reviewing of the elastic). Usually it is best to grant such decisions automatically rather than individually, by setting a credit line on the customer so that credit arising from individual transactions can be granted if the exposure falls within the credit line. However, the credit line originally established is based on credit information available at that time, and the credit manager must establish a procedure for the review of such information from time to time. This can be achieved by setting a credit line on a customer as to value and time, so that a review must occur to re-establish the line. The more undoubted the customer the longer can be the time before expiry of the line.

The information available to the credit manager at the time of original investigation, or review, can be classified according to whether it is obtained from internal or external sources.

7.31 Credit information from external sources

TRADE REFERENCES

A new customer will usually supply, on request, the names of two or more of his trade creditors who will give information to the supplier as to trade credit extended. While this source of information has advantages in being cheap and quick to obtain, it should be treated with care and used to extract the maximum amount of information. Caution is advised since the new customer may be selecting on a biased basis; he is unlikely to list the creditors that have had trouble in obtaining payment from him. Moreover, weight should be given to the information known on the company giving the reference and the opinions stated. A glowing reference from a sole trader that cannot be traced easily may just be too good to be true. Even a good reference from an established company may in fact refer to management that is no longer in control at the customer concerned.

Given the caution with which trade references should be treated, it is important to obtain maximum information from them. The credit manager should draw up a standard form of request for such information which, *inter alia*, should ask the highest credit granted by the supplier, whether payment terms have been adhered to and what those payment terms are, how long the trading relationship has been established, and any general comments to be given.

Satisfactory references from two or more suppliers should justify a low level of credit dependent upon the trading scale and pattern of the supplier.

Certainly it may not be worthwhile inquiring further for sums of less than £100 at any time.

BANK REFERENCES

To supplement trade references received, a supplier may inquire, through his bankers, of the client's bankers as to their opinion of the credit worth of the buyer. This is, again, a cheap method of obtaining information (the cost is rarely above £0·35) but it is in no way comprehensive. Enquiry should be for a specific, required amount and the credit term should be stated. Ambiguity should be absent. 'Is X Ltd. good for £750 credit?' can lead to an ambiguous answer. 'Is X Ltd. good for £750 credit outstanding at any one time, on 30 day credit terms?' should permit a specific reply.

The answer to a credit enquiry must be treated with caution. In many cases the customer may be attempting to act properly towards his bankers even if under pressure from his creditors. If the banker is having difficulty in operating the customer account and is attempting to put right an over-drawn situation, he is unlikely to give such a bad reference that credit is not extended to his customer.

To derive maximum value from a bank report or opinion, the recipient must be prepared to spend some time on its interpretation, to attempt to 'read between the lines' and to see into the mind of the writer. Certain standard phraseology will suggest, to the experienced interpreter, that all is not well. 'Your figure is higher than usually seen but do not think he would enter into commitments he would not fulfil', could mean that such risks are not usually taken by other creditors and possibly should not be taken. Similarly, 'considered good for your figure if in a series', could mean that credit of, say, £750 (requested) at any time is too high. 'Cannot speak for your figure', should mean keep off. Alternatively, 'undoubted for any amount' is unusually strong and can be relied upon to a large extent.

CREDIT AGENCIES

The credit manager can obtain reports from a credit bureau, on an individual basis, or purchase a credit register which will give basic information such as customer name and address, nature of business, capital, and average trade credit rating. In the former case each report may cost between £2·00 and £3·00 (far more for telephone or export enquiries) and, unless up-to-date information is on file at the bureau, three to four weeks can elapse before receipt.

The information contained in the report depends upon information available to the credit bureau. In some cases the bureau will attempt to interview the subject company to obtain information concerning sales, management and proprietors, and production. Furthermore, as both public and private companies must file Accounts for public review, it is possible for these figures to be included. In any event this could be obtained by the supplier from Company House. Regrettably many companies, at present, are very late in filing such Accounts, so that the information is often out of date. Additional information such as payment experience, trade credit granted, and any charges against the company's assets is also provided. In reviewing such reports, it is important to note the date prepared. Care should also be taken to select the appropriate agency for the trade and geographical area.

If credit enquiries must occur on a continuing basis, it could be worth-while paying a yearly subscription for a credit register listing the details of many thousands of customers. This register can be used as a guide and may be supplemented where necessary by an agency report. Again it is important to bear in mind the date the register was compiled.

7.32   Credit information from internal sources

Besides drawing information from third parties, the supplier can generate meaningful information from a number of its own departments. The useful-ness and desirability of this information is often very high.

REPRESENTATIVES' REPORTS

When attempting to open a new customer account, the sales representative will make a number of judgments. These he will not attempt to assemble in logical order, as they are subconsciously merged into answering the question, 'How much can I sell to this prospective customer?' Marshalled in proper order, the facts can assist in answering the question, 'How much should be sold to this prospective customer?' To marshal the facts, it is best to estab-lish a form for completion by the representative when opening a new account. Emphasis must be placed upon realistic completion of the form by the representative. There is no point in supplying more goods than can be sold by the customer before they are out of fashion, not fresh, or where goods must be sold before any payment, irrespective of terms, can be made. Completed information can be useful in initial appraisal of creditworthiness, especially when supplementing trade and bank references.

While information required will depend upon the trading activities and pattern of the supplier, the following information should normally be obtained:

(a) Correct name of business, and whether it is a limited company, partnership, or sole trader.

(b) Correct address, and whether a separate address is needed for payment of accounts.

(c) Whether there are any other branches in existence.

(d) General merchandise handled, and significance of supplier merchandise within overall sales.

(e) Whether competitors' goods are stocked.

(f) How much the customer could purchase in any week or month if the account is established, apart from amount of initial order.

(g) General comment as to proprietors, history, and general activity.

Direct Visits

In some countries, notably the United States, the customer is often happy to disclose financial information in order to secure large credit lines. This disclosure could be to credit agencies or even to important suppliers. This attitude has not yet prevailed in the United Kingdom; in fact until recently the opposite view was upheld. An Englishman's financial accounts, as well as his home, was his castle, and the walls were not to be breached. With the disclosure of financial information for public record now necessary, under the 1967 Companies Act, the greater emphasis upon disclosure of general information, and the recent failures of large companies, a more flexible attitude to the disclosure of financial information is beginning to appear.

Depending upon the relationship between supplier and customer, it is no longer impossible, although still a rare occurrence, for the supplier to suggest to the customer that the credit line contemplated (either as a new account, or an increase above the existing line) is such that a visit by the credit manager or accountant of the supplier to review available financial information would be desirable. In this way the supplier may obtain a review of audited accounts which are not yet a matter of public record, and sales and profitability may be discussed. This information can be extremely useful in allowing high credit exposures but can be used only in a minimal number of cases.

Sales Ledger Records

If the supplier is conducting continuing business with the customer, the sales ledger record with that customer will show the credit that has been extended and the manner in which the customer has met the obligation to pay on each due date. Many sources of credit information reviewed in this chapter are usually obtained at the commencement of a trading relationship. The one item missing is sales ledger information and care must be taken that this is incorporated into further reviews or increases of the credit line. One of the best guides to the changing strength of the elastic referred to earlier is the evidence unfolding in the sales ledger.

Table 7.1 shows four steps in the relationship between supplier and customer, and the effect of lack of continual credit control in reviewing payment experience.

1. Initial start of relationship. A credit limit of £750 is established assuming a general trade rating of £1,000, and goods to the value of £735 (after initial sample order) are supplied over a period of one month, on credit terms of payment at end of month following month of invoice.

2. Payment of the first group of invoices promptly (seven days after due date) and an increase in the credit line to £1,000, following upon prompt payment and no knowledge of a poor financial situation. Customer utilizes £900 of the credit line by further deliveries.

3. A deteriorating situation evidenced by payment of invoice 3223 twenty days after due date (as compared with seven days after due date in 2. above) and only payment on account of invoices 3313 and 3374 on October 15, such invoices being due on October 1. In the absence of other information to show a poor financial situation, the credit line of £1,000 is still maintained and utilized to £950 by further deliveries.

4. The final act. Under further pressure, and after stating he was not satisfied with the quality of merchandise (even though such complaints were not made at or shortly after receipt), the debtor makes a further payment on account on November 5. Even though the debtor is now 40 days overdue, the credit line has not been reduced and a further delivery of £250 is made on 10 November 1973, bringing the credit line of £1,000 to full use. A threat of legal action brings in a further payment of £100 on 29 November 1973, and at last the credit line is withdrawn (1 December 1973). Further requests for goods by the debtor are refused and despite promises to clear, in full, all overdue items (now totalling £650), of which £250 is more than 60 days overdue, only £50 is received on 20 December 1973. Legal action has to be taken. At this point the story ends, for the present, as sufficient experience has been reviewed for present purposes.

It is important to note that, even though other credit sources were not pointing to a deteriorating position, the story shown by the ledger record was clear. Prompt payment in August was followed by a slowing down of payment in September, with the first real warning sign showing on October 15 when part-payment only was made. Instead of reverting to a £750 credit line and keeping a careful watch on the position, a further delivery of £175 was allowed on October 28. Even though payment on account continued in

Table 7.1   SALES LEDGER RECORD: CUSTOMER LTD.

Date	Reference	Item	Due Date	Payment	Debit	Credit	Balance	
5. 6.73.	3092	Invoice	31. 7.73.	7. 8.73.	25·00	—	25·00	⎫
10. 6.73.	3100	Invoice	31. 7.73.	7. 8.73.	200·00		225·00	⎬ 1
27. 6.73.	3147	Invoice	31. 7.73.	7. 8.73.	360·00		585·00	
14. 7.73.	3223	Invoice	31. 8.73.	20. 9.73.	150·00		735·00	⎭
7. 8.73.	123	Cash	—	15.10.73.		585·00	150·00	⎫
18. 8.73.	3313	Invoice	30. 9.73.	5.11.73. Pt.	300·00		450·00	⎬ 2
22. 8.73.	3374	Invoice	30. 9.73.	5.11.73. Pt. 29.11.73. Pt. 20.12.73. Pt.	450·00		900·00	⎭
20. 9.73.	154	Cash	—	—		150·00	750·00	⎫
28. 9.73.	3513	Invoice	31.10.73.	—	225·00		975·00	⎬ 3
15.10.73.	192	Cash	—	—		200·00	775·00	
28.10.73.	3613	Invoice	30.11.73.	—	175·00		950·00	⎭
5.11.73.	202	Cash	—	—		200·00	750·00	⎫
10.11.73.	3694	Invoice	31.12.73.	—	250·00		1,000·00	⎬ 4
29.11.73.	271	Cash	—	—		100·00	900·00	
20.12.73.	301	Cash	—	—		50·00	850·00	⎭

LEGAL ACTION

early November and disputes were raised on an invoice more than two months old, the evidence was ignored, and the debtor, by now probably experiencing problems in obtaining supplies, uses the credit line to the maximum of £1,000. From this point continued collection pressure has some small effect and, too late, on December 1 the credit line is withdrawn. Even at this point further exposure is prevented by refusing further deliveries, and finally a balance of £850 is put into legal hands for collection.

The astute credit manager, while not avoiding loss, should have reduced the final balance considerably. A reversion to a credit line of £750 on October 15 would have prevented deliveries on October 28, and further on account payments on November 5 would have confirmed the possibility of loss, and led to withdrawal of credit facilities. Even if success in collection of the overdue invoices were no greater than shown, the final balance would have been £425, half of the loss suffered when the ledger experience was ignored.

This ending is not the only alternative. The credit manager might have allowed some deliveries against immediate cash payment to enable continuation of the debtor's business, and small repayment of the old outstanding invoices. Whatever the strategy used, the credit manager would be evaluating the facts from the ledger card to assist him in minimizing the loss, possibly ending in a figure of between £350 to £500.

One point is obvious; ignoring of ledger experience is the surest way of maximizing loss. Moreover, in a positive sense, if payment experience had continued as in 2. then this could have been used to increase credit lines gradually, over time, with the debtor allowing maximum sales based on good payment experience. Reinforced by updated information from other sources, the credit manager can answer, affirmatively, the question, 'How can more sales to this customer be allowed?' by referring to good payment experience. Naturally, as shown above, bad payment experience must be acted upon immediately if exposures beyond those normally spoken for are not to be turned into losses.

7.4　COLLECTION OF DEBTS

The main point of contact between the supplier's credit control department and the customer arises from collection activity. Success or failure in reconciling the objectives of minimizing, as far as possible, the cost of credit extended to the customer and of maintaining customer goodwill, will be determined by the actions of the collection department and the framework within which it operates, as set by the credit control policy.

In carrying out credit control policy, the collection department must be guided by two principles:

(a) Consistency in collection procedures.

(b) Flexibility in dealing with customers.

7.41 Consistency in collection procedures

In setting out credit control policy, selling and discount terms will be established, together with any internal level of tolerance to be granted past due date, when the customer can still be allowed to take cash discount. These, and the general collection procedures, will be set bearing in mind the following:

ESTABLISHED TERMS OF THE TRADE

As an example, in Britain it is usual for suppliers to the retail textile trade to offer a $3\frac{3}{4}$ per cent or 5 per cent cash discount for invoices paid within seven days, and $2\frac{1}{2}$ per cent cash discount if payment is made by the tenth of any month in respect of invoices dating from the nineteenth of the preceding month to the twentieth of the month before that preceding month. Suppliers not offering such discount may well find it being taken irrespective of their selling terms, thus leading to confusion.

STRENGTH OF SUPPLIER COMPARED WITH OTHER SUPPLIERS

If the supplier is operating within a very competitive supply situation, he will probably decide that normal collection procedures should not contemplate legal action until any debt is more than forty to fifty-five days overdue. The risk of losing a customer paying thirty days after due date is too great, if other suppliers are willing to allow this tolerance. However, if the products of the supplier are in some way superior to competitive articles, and much in demand, the period of forty to fifty-five days may be brought down to between thirty and forty days, and the time beyond stated date for cash discount allowance may be shortened from seven days to three days, or even one day.

The collection programme adopted should be related to the above criteria. Once adopted, it must be applied consistently in two ways. Firstly, if the aim is to reach taking legal action within, say, forty-five days past due date, then this should be upheld. There is no point in writing to a customer that is thirty-five days overdue stating that legal action will be taken if payment is not received within ten days, and then writing after a further fourteen days stating that payment is required immediately. If the first step has not been taken, why should the customer believe that any action will follow the further letter? Secondly, the programme agreed upon up to such point must be maintained, so that the customer has had adequate notice and warning of the position.

Assuming monthly account terms (all invoices dated in one month are due for payment at the end of the next month), a collection cycle could be settled as follows:

1. *Statement*

This will be sent on a monthly basis, showing customer indebtedness, immediately or as soon as possible after the close of the relevant 'base period'. In this case the base period is the calendar month, whereas in supplies to the British retail textile trade the base period would be the twentieth of one month to the nineteenth of the next month.

The statement will be used primarily as an informative document, allowing the customer to check and agree the items that will be due for payment at a later date, and thus such payment will be facilitated. However, it is also of use in showing the customer that certain items are overdue at the statement date, and should be paid.

Statements generally belong to one of two main categories: either those showing all items outstanding at a date, including overdue invoices, or those showing activity since the last statement, the final balance of which is shown as the opening balance on the present statement. Of the two categories, the 'open item' statement allows a detailed reconciliation of old items and is to be preferred. Both types of statement may attempt to analyze the overdue items into periods of time that the items are overdue (for example one month, two months, three months, and so on).

If an item falls overdue, then the statement can act as a first reminder, either implicitly by showing outstanding items or an uncleared balance brought forward from the preceding statement, or explicitly by a short note specifying that certain items are overdue and payment is awaited.

2. *First collection letter*

This could occur when the invoice is twenty days overdue. The letter should be a further reminder and as such should be courteous, rather than threatening. It should give details of what is required, if possible specifying the items that should be paid. Payment should be asked for as soon as possible, or the customer should be given a chance of stating why payment is not being made. Efforts should be made to see that this and later letters should not be stereotyped or 'depersonalized'. A letter that is not signed personally, or has clearly been produced by computer, or is repeated month after month, will not be taken seriously by a debtor wishing to extend his credit.

3. Second collection letter or telephone call

This may occur after a further fourteen days. The collection method used may vary according to the value of the debt outstanding. A policy may be laid down that items of more than £500 will be chased by direct telephone call, to ensure that there is no reason why the invoice should not be paid, and to obtain a specific promise of payment by certain date. If possible, such conversation should be confirmed by letter. The collection man making the call must be skilled at avoiding prevarication by the customer and must be able to reach the correct person in the purchase ledger department.

For overdue items of less than £500 a second letter may be sent. This should be more forceful, asking for immediate payment and stating the amount required. Reference may be made to the fact that previous reminders have not been answered.

4. Final letter or telephone call

If payment has not occurred after a further ten days, the invoice will be forty-four days overdue. Assuming that the supplier's administration is in no way at fault (either as to incorrect invoicing, delivery, or application of cash or invoices to the customer ledger card), clear action must be applied to limit the exposure on what might be a bad debt. By now the credit line and delivery authorization limit should have been reviewed, and the letter sent to the customer should be uncompromising.

The customer must be made aware that if payment is not received within, say, seven days from date of letter, then immediate action will be taken to recover the debt by any method thought necessary, including legal action. The amount that is long overdue should be stated clearly, and payment should also be requested for items which may now be fourteen days overdue. It may be that the letter should be signed by a senior executive, possibly the credit manager, chief accountant, or company secretary, to emphasize the serious intent of the supplier.

If the amount is deemed to be serious, a telephone call may be useful to emphasize the situation to the customer. This should be confirmed in writing. Having made the customer aware that final action will be taken if payment is not received, the supplier must take such action in the absence of such payment.

5. Final action

Unless the supplier is of a substantial size, it will not have its own legal department to process legal action against debtors. In any event it may not wish to use its legal department for such purposes. The usual choice, after the final letter has not produced a satisfactory result, is between the use of a debt collection agency (often useful in certain industries or trades) or an outside solicitor. If the latter course is chosen, care should be taken to review the operations of the solicitor to see that he can cope administratively with the number of cases that may be passed to him.

The process of legal proceedings necessary to obtain payment (if any is possible), involving the issue of a summons or writ, and proceeding through the courts to obtain judgment, after which realization of available assets by various methods can occur, is complex and outside the scope of this review of the internal functions of the supplier's credit control department. However, where final action is being conducted it is best to remove this debtor from the general ledger and out of the jurisdiction of the credit manager, as this would detract from control of current credit transactions. The debtor position should be passed to the chief accountant or company secretary, and whoever is now responsible for final realization must work closely with the relevant debt collection agency or solicitor, ensuring that he reviews the action being taken by them on a regular basis. Even if a debt collection agency is chosen in the first place, it may eventually be necessary to effect legal action through solicitors.

7.42 Flexibility in dealing with customers

The principle of consistency must not be confused with rigidity. In every spread of customers, there are usually 'special situations' which must fall outside the normal collection process, and allowance must be made for this fact.

The major problems facing the credit manager in this area are those customers that, by virtue of their special market position and strength, negotiate high cash discounts for short payment terms, or longer payment than is usual, for example, sixty or ninety days. Such customers must be removed from the normal collection process. The customer paying on ninety days should not receive reminder letters on a monthly account cycle basis, and the collection process after due date should cover a much shorter period since longer terms have been extended.

A further problem is the customer taking very heavy supplies up to the maximum credit limit allotted to his account. In this case special arrangements may be entered into to ensure that the limit is not exceeded, by payments being made, even on or before due date of invoices, prior to further deliveries occurring. This calls for special control of such accounts, and normal routines will not be sufficient for such customers.

Finally, the very large customer of 'undoubted' credit standing may require special handling. In some cases such companies take extended credit either deliberately or through sheer volume of total purchases, giving rise to administrative problems. Here the credit manager must attempt to locate the person responsible for making payments on his account. The establishing of a personal relationship, either through phone calls or visits, may be well worthwhile in limiting the credit extended on such accounts.

In all 'special' cases the normal collection process may be waived with good results. The blending of the flexible approach with consistency in procedures covering 'normal' situations, is often the best way to limit credit extended without loss of goodwill.

Part Three: Factoring Examined

8 Factoring – What it Means

8.1 FACTORING DEFINED

The distinguishing characteristics of factoring emanate from the lack of obligations of the client after transfer of the debt to the factor, and the resulting services performed by the factor. The historical survey of factoring shows that the factor evolved in America as a purchaser of trade debts without recourse to the client in the event of customer inability to pay, carrying out all functions necessary to receive payment of such debts from customers. While a small, but important, minority of factors in the United Kingdom purchase debts with recourse to the client, this is outside the mainstream of the development of factoring as generally practised, since the financial effect of purchasing debts with full recourse is equivalent to an invoice discounting facility (or, in America, an accounts receivable financing programme). However, disclosure to the customer allows many services associated with a factoring facility to be performed.

In treating the purchasing of debts with recourse as being outside the general mainstream of factoring, factoring can be defined as involving the purchase of debts from a client by the factor, without recourse to the client by the factor in the event of a customer being unable to pay, with notification to all customers informing them that the factor has acquired the account and that payment should be made directly to the factor.

Payment by the factor for debts purchased, or the obligation to pay, can occur either substantially at the date of purchase of the book debt, the client enjoying an 'old line' or 'full' factoring facility, or on an agreed due date, the client enjoying a 'maturity' factoring facility. For both facilities a service fee is charged expressed as a percentage of sales, while under an 'old line' facility a payment made prior to agreed due date of the invoice will bear a charge based on the value and term of such payment. In no way can factoring be equated with loans against the security of book debts, as in invoice discounting operations.

While both facilities have their proper role to play in the expansion of trade, the distinguishing characteristics of factoring, namely outright purchase of debts allowing 100 per cent credit protection against any bad debts, and the provision of services allowing for direct collection of all debts, set it apart from forms of book debt financing practised in the United Kingdom today.

8.2 RANGE OF SERVICES OFFERED

The definition of a factoring facility shows a clear delineation between the administrative and financial services offered by the factor. The administrative service is enjoyed by the client whether he requests an 'old line' or 'maturity' facility. However, the financial service varies according to the type of facility extended.

The administrative service is grouped into four sections, each of which is designed to contribute to the final aim of the factor in collecting, in full, debts purchased from the client at 100 per cent of their face value. To achieve this objective, the client should be selling goods and/or services to credit-worthy customers, raising invoices correctly (in that all necessary ancillary procedures should have been carried out), and adopting proper accounting and collection procedures. The factoring services arise directly from the legal position of the factor as a purchaser of debts without recourse, and his desire to collect such debts.

8.21 Credit assessment and protection against non-payment by customers

The factor will undertake all procedures usual in establishing credit lines or limits up to which the client may trade with each customer, and will take 100 per cent of the loss arising from the customer's inability to pay, where such loss falls within the credit line granted by the factor. The factor will carry out at his own cost the gathering of information necessary for credit decisions to be taken, such as the obtaining of credit agency reports, trade credit registers for reference, bank and trade references, company searches, and reports of the factoring credit executive who may visit the client.

His ability to grant 100 per cent credit protection, once the credit line has been established by the review of the factor's credit assessor, partly arises from the direct control of the asset that the factor enjoys. This control is in many cases exercised simultaneously through another of the factor's clients.

The further cost of continually updating credit information on each customer is also undertaken by the factor, and this will form the basis of any amendments to credit lines or limits he may advise to the client.

8.22 Maintenance of a detailed sales ledger

Since the client is selling debts to the factor at full face value, without recourse in the event of customer failure to pay, it is necessary for the factor to maintain a record of these debts in such a way that he can obtain payment as soon as possible. The factor will maintain a record of book debts purchased, updating this by reference to cash received, credit notes, and further invoices, divided according to customer in such a way as to allow information to be used efficiently in the collection process. The client will have one sales ledger account with the factor.

8.23 Collection of all book debts purchased from the client

In collecting all book debts when due for payment, the factor is extinguishing his own possible loss, not simply carrying out a service on behalf of the client. The factor will obtain relevant information from his own sales ledger and send out monthly statements of account to customers where necessary, following this with collection letters, personal collection control, and legal action if necessary. All legal costs in attempting collection on debts purchased without recourse are borne by the factor. The degree of liaison between the factor and client in undertaking this activity will be reviewed in Chapter 9.

8.24 Ancillary administrative services

The services rendered by the factor in this area are neither essential nor offered by all factors. Nevertheless, many factors undertake certain functions, for the benefit of both client and factor, to check that the client is carrying out procedures necessary to ensure that the debt purchased by the factor is valid and enforceable, and that queries will not arise at the collection stage. The factor may send staff to the client to review control procedures and documentation, to ensure correct contracting and invoicing, quality control, despatch of merchandise, and handling of any returns, all aimed at minimizing delays in settlement. This will tend to lead to a close relationship with the client, allowing him to discuss his commercial development with an informed third party.

8.25 The financial service

The financial service offered by the factor under a 'maturity' factoring facility is that of guaranteed date of payment to the client of debts purchased on a without recourse basis, subject to such debts not being disputed by the customer. The calculation of the guaranteed payment date by the factor will take into account previous ledger experience and a period for slow collection after due date of invoice.

This facility differs from a factoring facility where advances against book debts are not made, and the factor pays the client upon receiving payment from the customer. The latter case is not a 'maturity' facility, but one with a requirement by the factor that 100 per cent reserve be maintained at all times. The client, in this case, has no guaranteed payment date, although the factor should speed up the process of collection for the benefit of the client, by applying agreed policies consistently.

Under an 'old line' facility the factor is providing the financial service of allowing the client greater velocity of working capital, in making part-payment for debts purchased at their full face value immediately upon purchase. A charge is rendered on such part-payment, from the time of such payment to the anticipated date of receipt of the book debts purchased. Alternatively, the charge may run to date of actual collection if an estimated credit period cannot be established. Final payment of the balance for book debts purchased occurs on collection or the agreed maturity date.

8.3 ADMINISTRATION BETWEEN CLIENT AND FACTOR

While the administrative services performed by the factor relieve the client of the day-to-day tasks necessary to effect a proper system of credit control, it is a mistake to assume that a factor can remove the problems arising from incorrect performance, actual or alleged, of the sales contract by the client, due either to incorrect time or place of delivery, or to quality and quantity of merchandise delivered. Similarly, while numerous sales ledgers have been replaced by one ledger, the factor's account in the ledger of the client, this individual ledger with the factor is ignored by the client at his peril.

To realize the maximum benefit from a factoring relationship, the client must ensure an efficient reporting and checking system with the factor. In fact, it is often advisable for him to appoint a factoring liaison officer in his company, with the responsibility for the smooth control of and reaction to all information emanating from the factoring relationship.

Particular points to be kept under constant scrutiny by the client include the following:

8.31 Factoring credit lines

As far as possible sales to customers should be made within the factoring credit lines established. The factor, in checking credit lines, has taken into account the trading requirements of the client, and if restricted credit lines have been established there should be good reason for this decision. The factor is concerned to grant as much credit cover as is possible, so that any loss is for his own account, and will have good reason for not meeting his client's requirements.

Sales made above the credit lines set can cause an overtrading situation to develop, causing consequential problems in collection. Similarly, a very large order can mean that the customer cannot obtain credit elsewhere or, in the case of a retail outlet, heavy overstocking can mean that payment, whatever the payment terms, can only be effected as, and if, goods are sold.

Constant breaching of the credit line set by the factor normally leads to an increase in the average credit period, a high dispute and returns ratio, and additional work for the factor and client, with both parties becoming frustrated. The factor is carrying out more work than is normal for the volume of sales conducted, and the client finds the benefits of administrative service and financial availability reduced, when the factor becomes restrictive in his approach to such a facility.

8.32 Schedules of invoices

Schedules of invoices should be sent to the factor after the proper performance of the sales contract by delivery of goods or rendering of services. Invoices should contain all information necessary for the purchaser to effect prompt payment, such as consignment address, customer order number, method and date of delivery, terms of payment, correct calculations, and value-added tax details. The notation required by the factor should be detailed upon each invoice.

8.33 Disputes concerning payment

In attempting collection, the factor will from time to time receive reasons for non-payment or reduced payment by the customer. In this case, the factor will refer the dispute to the client, and it is essential that prompt attention is given to the dispute, and a comprehensive and detailed reply sent to the factor, thus allowing the customer to be contacted. Although the factor is not liable for any loss arising from disputes, he will often attempt to collect according to the client's explanation. If the dispute continues the factor will eventually pass the debt back to the client, but in many cases payment can be obtained after clarification with the customer by the factor.

Lack of proper and prompt response by the client to notices of dispute, or delay in issuing credit notes when due, can have a disastrous effect upon the relationships created by the factoring agreement. The good customer raising a valid query will be frustrated by the apparent lack of attention to such queries and may reduce purchases from the supplier. A customer seeking to avoid or delay payment will become aware that the raising of frivolous disputes will postpone payment and cause confusion between client and factor.

8.34 Factor's accounts

At regular intervals, usually monthly, the factor will send a report to the client covering all transactions since the end of the previous period. Schedules of invoices or credit notes factored, and payments against invoices, will be detailed. Other debits (for example, factoring service fee, charges for payments prior to invoice maturity dates, and debts under dispute transferred to the client) will be shown, as will the effect of all transactions on the balance due to the client. To prevent misunderstanding between the client and the factor and lack of collection activity, either by client or factor, the client should check all entries in his account.

The administrative process between the client and the factor revolves around the points discussed above. The client will request credit lines to be established on all customers, expressed either as an amount outstanding at any time, or an amount to be shipped within a certain period, or an amount to be covered in a single shipment.

The factor will confirm to the client whether such a request is granted, after which the client can deliver goods, or render services, up to the established line, and sell the resulting invoice or invoices to the factor without being responsible for loss due to the financial failure of the customer. All such invoices will be detailed by schedule to the factor, a copy of this schedule, retained by the client, representing the sales day book of the client.

Detailed sales ledger work after this time is carried out by the factor, who will revert to the client only if a customer disputes an invoice. If a dispute cannot be cleared, it will become the responsibility of the client.

Although the factor owns all debts, it is usual to send the client information on these as the client has a commercial interest in continuing business with the customers, and therefore should be aware of collection action being taken and any amounts overdue.

The client will receive 100 per cent credit for book debts upon purchase, and payment will be made according to the terms of the individual factoring agreement. Upon receipt of the factor's account with him, he should check all entries to ensure agreement between his control sales ledger and the balance shown by the factor, adjusting any errors that may have occurred.

8.4 THE VALUE OF THE FACTORING SERVICE

During the 1960s factoring, in the United Kingdom, became known as a financial service for companies that were unable to obtain financial accommodation from their banks. An educational process is still in hand to convince industry and commerce that this is an incorrect view. While the financial benefits can be paramount in certain situations, many of the long-term and worthwhile relationships between factor and client exist because the true benefits of the administrative service, and the consequent release of senior management time, have become apparent to the client.

In essence, factoring is a means of 'sub-contracting out' certain management tasks to a specialist organization, allowing management to concentrate on the task of increasing profitability, normally through increased efficiency in marketing or production. The positive reasons for requesting a factoring facility, being a wish to use working capital more productively to allow for increased production, a desire for greater efficiency in management control, embracing financial planning and concentration of profitmaking activities, and realization of potential marketing situations, point to its value for forward-looking management.

The factor faced with a request that is intended to stave off the evil day of receivership or liquidation should realize that factoring, in these circumstances, is not providing a service either to the client or to those with whom he has business dealings.

9 Administrative Services Covered

9.1 CREDIT ASSESSMENT AND PROTECTION AGAINST BAD DEBTS

9.11 British and American practice

For nearly all factors in the United Kingdom, the ability to grant protection against customer bad debts for the client is at the centre of the 'full' factoring facility. In the United States, the granting of protection against customer bad debts is the distinguishing feature of factoring, when compared to any other financial or management facility. 'Factoring is the outright sale of accounts receivables without recourse.'* This view is held throughout American factoring literature. 'In technical terms, the distinguishing feature of the old line factoring (hereinafter called "factoring") arrangement is the purchase by the factor of the receivables of its client without recourse to the factored client for any financial inability of the account debtor to pay.'†

Table 3.2 shows that nearly all British factors offer without recourse factoring to their clients. It is the ability of the factor to grant protection against customer bad debts that allows him not to view the client as a borrower of his funds, and the credit department of the factor is central to this attitude. The ability of the factor to protect his client against customer bad debts will depend upon the skill and experience of the personnel in the credit department. They will introduce a systematic approach in this area for the client, and will rely upon the normal sources of knowledge as well as specialized information that is not available outside the factoring office.

The development of the American factoring industry in the textile field shaped the development of the credit departments of the factors. The credit department was essentially split into two sections, wholesale, approving credits on manufacturers and distributors, and retail, approving credits on department stores, chains, or individual shops. Within each section the

---

* I. Naitove, *Modern Factoring* (American Management Association Inc. 1969) p. 18.
† R. Martin, *Commercial Financing*, ed., M. R. Lazere (The Ronald Press Co. 1968), p. 73.

credit assessor, or credit man, would have graded levels of responsibility and, consequent upon the structure of trade, it was normal that the higher levels of credit responsibility were to be found in the wholesale section, as this involved the reviewing of larger customers. The rise of department stores blurred this distinction, and British factors have not followed this method of organization.

The British factoring industry has developed across a very wide range of manufacturing and distributive trades, and credit assessors generally develop a specialized knowledge in certain industries. However the factoring credit department is organized, the attitude of the credit assessor is to attempt to approve the credit requested by the client, rather than to avoid all possibility of bad debt loss. This attitude derives from the fact that the factor receives income in direct relation to the volume of sales purchased from its clients. To the extent that the factor cannot grant credit protection on individual customers, so the facility may become more restrictive and may eventually cease, and in any event relations between the client and the factor become difficult. This is not to say that the factor will grant credit protection against unreasonable requirements, but that the credit man does not expect to avoid all customer bad debt losses, which would result only from an extremely restrictive credit policy.

9.12 Methods of granting protection against bad debts

The factor will use two basic methods of approach in granting protection against bad debts, the appropriate method being decided by the nature of trading of the client.

CREDIT LINES OR CREDIT LIMITS

Upon request by the client, the factor will establish a line of credit up to which the client can sell to the customer. This line or limit will refer to the value outstanding at any time over a fixed period, to allow for regular review at the end of each such period, or until withdrawn. The amount outstanding at any time that the factor would cover is related to the needs of the client rather than to the credit standing of the customer. A client selling £1,000 per month to Imperial Chemical Industries Ltd. would not wish to receive credit cover of £100,000 at any time from the factor on this customer, even though the customer is undoubted.

As the client has handed over the sales ledger operation to the factor, he must overcome the problem of ensuring that goods shipped are within the credit line established. This problem can be overcome by a variety of methods.

The factor may establish for the client a monthly sales figure for the customer, which will be covered automatically within the credit line established, so that the client can deliver goods in the knowledge that such shipments are automatically covered. For example, a client selling on strict sixty-day terms will receive a monthly shipping limit of £1,000 on a customer, if the factor has granted a credit line of £2,500 for the customer and is allowing some fifteen days for collection after due date. Alternatively, the factor may allow small shipments to be covered automatically, irrespective of the credit line granted on the individual customer.

In many cases, the factor may provide the client with customer account information, for example by means of a regular ageing of accounts, which will allow the client to review the position on various customers, even though the sales ledger operation is being maintained by the factor. In this way the client has the ability to view the position of each customer before any large shipments are made. In any case, the client is able to contact the factor at any time for information on the up-to-date position on any customer account.

The method of establishing credit lines or credit limits, where the factor sets a maximum limit related to customer standing, rather than a line relating to client need, is suitable in situations where shipments are made at very frequent intervals to customers, and are usually of fairly small values.

Order or Shipment Approvals

Where larger deliveries are involved, and where the industry itself may be of a volatile nature, both parties may prefer the client to obtain credit cover from the factor on an order or shipment basis. The client will contact the factor by phone or telex, giving details as to the customer and the proposed delivery, value, credit terms, and delivery dates. The credit man will review the customer information and approve such requests on a specific basis, allocating an approval number which will be followed through in resulting documentation raised by the client. The factoring department will usually work on a daily approval sheet for each client, and a copy of this sheet will be sent to the client confirming the decisions taken during the day.

The speed with which the credit man can approve or reject requests from the client will depend upon the information at hand, and may take no more than five minutes in many cases, but where a new customer is involved on which the factor does not have information, there may be a delay of several days. The approval given by the factor to the individual requests can be telephoned to the client immediately if required, and if necessary may even be given to the client as soon as requested.

INFORMATION AVAILABLE TO THE CREDIT ASSESSOR

General Information

Whether the credit line or order approval method is used, the credit assessor will refer to the same basic information, as listed below. In some cases that information will also be available to credit assessors of individual large suppliers:

1. Credit registers would be referred to, such as Dun & Bradstreet, in order to obtain immediate rating on the customer.
2. Credit agency reports would be taken out where appropriate so as to obtain general information.
3. Bank reports and trade references would be obtained, again the credit man deciding whether or not these would be required.
4. This could be supplemented by searches being made through the company register to obtain information that is detailed and made available by law.

Specialist information

In obtaining and reviewing the above information, the credit assessor would be using his specialized knowledge in interpretation and collating of information, but would not be in a different position from his counterpart in the offices of the large supplier. However, he can then proceed to refer to the information that is specific to the factor, namely total prior trading experience with the customer. The factor will be able to review specific trading experience to analyze the trend of credit taken by the customer, and the efficiency with which individual items are paid, and to relate that experience to the present request.

If the factor is acting on behalf of a number of clients supplying to the particular customer, then he may well approach that customer, with the clients' agreement, in order to obtain more information to see if the credit requests are reasonable in relation to the business being conducted. This may mean that the credit man will visit the premises of the customer, discuss his present trading situation and volume, and review future prospects.

While this practice is still a rare occurrence in Britain, it is quite usual in America for the credit man of the factoring company to act in this way. The credit man is adopting a positive attitude in trying to justify the credit requests of the client or clients, and the attitude of customers in Britain is changing in relation to this positive approach, since by discussing their requirements with the credit man customers may obtain greater overall lines of credit from the factor's clients.

9.13   Client risk or department risk sales

DEFINITION OF TERMS

Sales which the factor purchases from the client without granting protection against customer bad debt are known as client risk, department risk, or with recourse sales.

The term 'client risk' is self-explanatory, while the term 'department risk' relates to the development of the factoring industry in America. To allow for rapid communication between the sales department of the client and the credit department of the factor, it was a normal practice for the factors, at the end of the nineteenth century and beginning of the twentieth century, to sublet a portion of their offices to the sales office of the client. The sales offices were departments of the client and if they agreed to ship goods even though the factor could not approve credit, the resulting sales would be conducted at department (or client) risk.

The practice of the factor subletting his premises to the sales department of the client has now ceased, due to the improvement in methods of rapid communication between client and factor. The term 'department risk' is still used on some occasions and denotes client risk sales.

'With recourse sales' again refers to those sales of the client that have not been approved by the factor, so that the factor has recourse to the client in the event of the customer's inability to pay.

THE FACTOR'S ATTITUDE TO CLIENT RISK SALES

Factors in the United Kingdom vary in their approach to the handling of client risk sales. In some cases availability of funds is only granted against sales purchased and approved by the factor, client risk sales being purchased by the factor without any funds being made available against such purchases, and the factor paying the client only upon collection from the customer.

However, some factors will review the value of such client risk sales and will continue to make an agreed availability of funds against all sales purchased, client or factor risk sales. In this situation the factor will constantly review the total position of client risk sales, often by means of fairly sophisticated accounting equipment. The factor is concerned as to the percentage of total debts outstanding at client risk, and the concentration within that percentage. This will affect his view of the overall facility and may lead him to reduce the overall availability to the client, or to introduce a restriction of availability against client risk sales.

EXAMPLE OF COMPARATIVE CLIENT RECOURSE LISTINGS

In the two situations set out in Table 9.1, the factor will be happier in the first situation where, even though the overall recourse represents 15 per cent

Table 9.1

COMPARATIVE CLIENT RECOURSE LISTINGS

EXAMPLE 1

Customer	Recourse (£)	Reasons for Recourse
A Ltd.	500	Credit declined
B Ltd.	300	Excess over maximum limit
C Ltd	1,000	Excess over credit line
D Ltd.	1,200	Excess over maximum limit
,,	,,	
,,	,,	
,,	,,	
N Ltd.	900	No limit. Prior invoice overdue
O Ltd.	2,000	Excess over credit line
15 customers	£15,000	Total recourse (15%)
	£100,000	Total debtors outstanding

EXAMPLE 2

P Ltd.	6,000	Credit declined
Q Ltd.	4,000	Credit declined
2 customers	£10,000	Total recourse (10%)
	£100,000	Total debtors outstanding

of total debts outstanding, this is well spread between some fifteen customers. In the second situation, even though the percentage of client risk sales is only 10 per cent of sales outstanding, nevertheless this is concentrated into two large accounts on which the factor feels he is unable to grant any protection against bad debts. If these two customer accounts were to cease to trade and were unable to make payments to creditors, then recourse into the client by the factor would be of a very serious nature. It is in such situations of concentration of risk that the factor becomes concerned with the client facility. Because of this concern, it is obvious that the collection efforts of the factor will be directed very heavily at the individual large client risk concentrations.

The table shows that the factor is not only concerned with percentages and concentrations but also with the reasons for such concentration. The factor may pay less attention to client risk sales which may have arisen through inefficiency of the client in making credit approval applications, as compared with other situations detailed in the table. Generally, exceeding of credit lines as opposed to maximum credit limits is not viewed with the same seriousness by the factor. The factor may well be able to increase the credit line on any customer if the trading experience of the client shows that this is required. Again, a situation where the factor has specifically declined or withdrawn credit, due to bad operating experience with the customer in respect of other client facilities, means that the factor will view any concentration into these customers with such seriousness that a lowering of availability of funds, either on a general or specific customer basis, may result.

9.14 Summary

The factor has therefore added to the general services of a credit control and protection department that the client may establish in his own offices by the use of skilled and experienced personnel related to the level of credit decisions taken. Moreover, it can draw upon operating experience on all customers for all clients, and may be able to develop more information on each customer than could any individual client. The use of these very specialized services, allied to sophisticated output of data from the factor's offices, means that the client is enjoying, in many cases, a credit department that he could not establish himself. A factor offering a flexible and up-to-date credit service to his client should be able to work with the client to increase client sales, but at the same time guide the client away from potentially difficult and dangerous situations before any large involvement arises.

9.2 SALES LEDGER CONTROL

9.21 Object of sales ledger control

The sales ledger control functions undertaken by the factor are not intended to duplicate the functions of the client, but rather to carry out the prime input and update functions for the detailed customer ledgers, so that effective credit and collection activities may be carried out by the factor, without reference to the client for additional information.

The factor will face the same basic problems of sales ledger control as will the client, in the absence of a factoring agreement. The factor normally has an advantage in that the size of his operation, overall, allows him to make use of sophisticated input, storage, and information retrieval equipment. In all cases, the object will be to process and store information so as to allow for a review of customer payment experience, thus assisting credit decisions, and further to allow for systematic and up-to-date collection activity. The information contained in the sales ledger for each client must therefore be up-to-date, readily obtainable, and accurate.

9.22   Choice of a sales ledger system

In maintaining the sales ledger for each client, the factor will make a basic decision to follow the principles of one of two systems.

THE BALANCING METHOD

Under this system transactions by customer are regarded in chronological order of events, with a balance being struck and carried forward, normally at monthly intervals. Collection activity is geared to balances brought forward and cash is not allocated against individual open items.

THE OPEN ITEM METHOD

Under this system all cash and other credits that are received are identified and matched against specific invoices. Thus it is always possible to reconcile the balance on the customer account into the various open items that are still outstanding.

The second method is used by many factors as it allows collection activity to occur on identifiable debts, and credit activity to function more properly as payment is related to specific open items. However, it is necessary for the factor to be able to maintain a historical record or analysis of such payments, rather than allow items simply to be deleted from a computer record when paid. This can be overcome by additional programming, allowing the computer to review the historical payment record on each customer. Alternatively, if bookkeeping machines are in use, the ledger card itself can be referred to for payment experience.

9.23   Example of standard sales ledger procedure

Table 9.2 shows an example of a standard ledger card and in this case the invoice, when cleared, has been detailed as to date of clearance. This allows the credit assessor to review a complete picture of payment record on the account at one glance. The advantages of using sophisticated equipment to control the sales ledger operation are also obvious, in that time-consuming operations such as preparation of statements and initial collection letters, analysis of debtors ledger as to items overdue, and other management

Table 9.2   SAMPLE SALES LEDGER CARD

Account No. ....

Name ....

Address ....

Credit Line ....

Terms ....

Date	Details	Cleared	Debit	Credit	Balance
28.11.72.	INV 3017	12. 1.73.	150-30		150-30
2.12.72.	INV 4917	10. 2.73.	53-11		203-41
5.12.72.	INV 5002	10. 2.73.	200-42		403-83
27.12.72.	CN 112	—		11-31	392-52
12. 1.73.	CSH 20	—		138-99	253-53
28. 1.73.	INV 5993		137-32		390-85
10. 2.73.	CSH 25			253-53	137-32

information can be produced extremely quickly, allowing various other functions to be carried out more efficiently.

INPUT DATA FOR THE SALES LEDGER

The factor will receive the prime data for input from two sources, namely client and debtor. The client will send to the factor, at agreed intervals, schedules of invoices backed by copies of such invoices and the original invoices if so required. Once the factor has accepted these invoices and has proved them arithmetically to the schedules, the individual invoices will be used as primary posting data in order to provide input for the sales ledger. This information will be transferred on to individual ledger cards, tape or other storage facility for computer purposes, depending upon the equipment used by the factor. Individual customer accounts will be debited, while the client will be credited in total with the value of invoices received. The original invoice that is sent to the customer, either direct from the client or via the factor, will bear a notation that the invoice has been purchased by the factor and that the debt, when due, should be paid direct to that factor.

Therefore the factor will be receiving a stream of payments from various customers and will be allocating those payments to the individual customer ledger. The cash sheets produced by the factor will again be used as primary posting data for input and update of the sales ledger. If the factor is operating an open item sales ledger system, he will attempt to allocate each cash item to the specific open items on the relevant customer account.

If this cannot be done the customer would normally be asked for more information, and only as a last resort will the factor use the right to allocate payments against the earliest items still outstanding. All cash received by the factor will be credited to the individual customers and debited to the cash receipts of the factoring company. The client has received full credit for invoices at the time of their submission to the factor.

While invoices and cash receipts are the two main categories of input data to the sales ledger, other data will be received from time to time in particular credit notes received from the client credited to the customer and debited to the client's account, and other adjustments such as items passed back to the client should they be in dispute for any long period of time.

The key to the undertaking of these operations by the factor is his direct and disclosed relationship with the customers of the client. For this reason, the prime data can be processed by the factor, so that the client's work is restricted to the raising of invoices and scheduling of such invoices to the factor. All other information and processing is carried out, from that time, by the factor. The client has replaced numerous accounts with one account due the client, namely the factor. The changed position resulting from the factoring arrangement, as regards the flow of debts, funds to the client, and payments by customers is shown in Figure 9.1.

9.3 COLLECTION

The undertaking of the collection function by the factor is possible because of notification to the customer by the client that each invoice is payable to the factor, and the maintaining of detailed customer ledger records by the factor. The factor's collection department is often divided so as to allocate responsibility for collection on certain client ledgers, or groups of customers, to various collection men, who will operate or supervise the collection activity for those clients or customers. The collection man normally operates on a separate basis from the credit man, but will work closely with him if a particular customer account becomes difficult to collect, or conversely if adverse credit information becomes available to the credit department.

The collection man will aim to attain firm and consistent, but not inflexible, collection procedures. On the one hand, he is aware that incorrect handling of the collection activity may prejudice the relationship between the client and the customer, to the detriment of both client and factor (the former losing sales, the latter losing factoring income). On the other, he knows that the sole asset of the factor is the total of debts purchased from clients, and that it is the function of the collection department to ensure that collection, or the obtaining of the reason for non-collection, is accomplished.

9.31 Relationship between client, customer, and factor

Far from injuring the relationship between client and customer, there are many reasons why the presence of the factor should improve the position. The factor will aim at increasing the client's sales, to derive increased factoring commission income, and the loss of sales to a customer upset by heavy-handed collection procedures is contrary to this objective. Moreover, factors operate within a competitive service industry, and disruption by the factor of the sales relationship could lead to the loss of that client to another factor. The factor's attitude, therefore, while being firm and consistent, is not such as to create offence except to those customers not wishing to pay in any event, or only after extremely extended credit.

At the same time, there are advantages for the customer arising from the interposition of the factor in the collection process. For various reasons the payment process of the customer, which in any event is often divorced

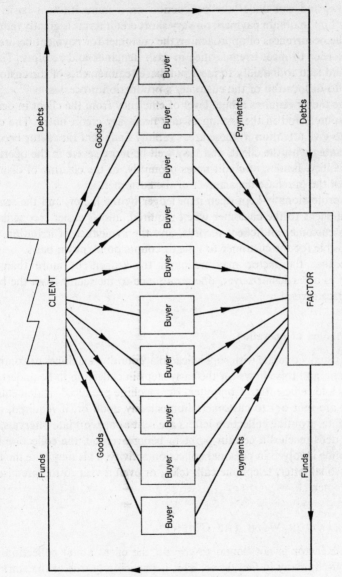

FIGURE 9.1. Relationships of client, customer, and factor.

from the purchasing process, may be assisted, particularly where the client of the factor is of no more than medium size.

1. The small supplier is able to plan development within a more certain cash flow, and can undertake production on a more rational basis. The need for him to obtain payment on very short credit terms is greatly reduced, as are the occurrences of approaching the customer for payment before due date in order to meet irregularities in cash demands and receipts. This in turn could lead to inability to meet purchase requirements of the customer, leading to dislocation of the customer's production processes.

2. The factor requires a high level of efficiency from the client in dealing with disputes, and in the issuing of any necessary credit notes. The client failing to give attention to these areas rapidly finds that the factor becomes disenchanted with the client, and may well be more severe in the operation of the facility. Issuing of credit notes promptly, or the clearing of disputes, will assist the purchase department of the customer.

3. A professionally-kept open item ledger by the factor, and the sending of a statement to the customer when required, allows easier reconciliation between customer and client records, and the avoidance of irritation. It is also possible for the customer to take discounts on a known basis.

4. Because the factor may maintain the ledgers of more than one supplier to a particular buyer, one remittance to the factor from the buyer can replace several.

9.32   Method of operation

Factors usually operate with sophisticated accounting machines or computer equipment, and this allows for the early steps in collection to be undertaken quickly and efficiently. Computer or machine-produced statements of account are sent out to customers immediately upon or, if required, prior to due date. Routine collection letters are sent at appropriate intervals, and when a debt reaches a certain point in being overdue, the collection man will become involved in personal collection activity. This may take the form of a personal letter, telephone call, telex, or even a visit to the premises of the customer.

CONSULTATION WITH THE CLIENT

While the factor is not bound to consult the client about collection procedures used, many in fact do so. This is particularly true at the start of a factoring relationship as to the time-scale of the collection process to legal action, consultation with the client prior to irrevocable action being taken, and the policy on cash discounts to be allowed. The amount of information given by the factor to the client as to the position on collections throughout the factoring facility varies considerably, but many feel that the client, although not owning the book debt, should be aware of the exact collection position, as this can affect current sales situations. The collection man will work from management information and reviews of individual collection files, in the handling of the client's ledger.

DEBTORS AGEING SUMMARY

One important review of the client position is the debtors ageing summary often produced monthly. This is an analysis of the total trade debts outstanding on a client's sales ledger, by customer and length of time each open item is overdue past settlement date. A typical ageing summary is shown in Table 9.3. This allows the collection man to see at a glance the larger concentrations falling past due and, by reference to credit information and updating of cash receipts, he can direct his activities into the areas of exposure. For example, the routine procedures involved when invoices are only just past due may be bypassed if the invoice is extremely large, or customer credit standing uncertain, and personal collection activity may be undertaken immediately.

The ageing summary can be used by senior management of the factor to review collection activity on a management by exception basis, and could also be used by the client as a point of reference for requests as to the collection position on any individual debtor. Any items more than ninety days overdue should be reviewed individually, and should either be the subject of legal action, or a technical dispute, or should be reviewed as a possible bad debt to be written off to the factor's bad debt reserve.

DISPUTES BETWEEN CLIENT AND CUSTOMER

In undertaking collection activity, the factor will bring to light disputes between client and customer, debtor accounts becoming overdue because of refusal to pay. Disputes also become known to the factor through cash allocation department, as many customers will state the reasons for part-payment on the remittance advice slip to the factor. The collection department must be aware of all customer disputes so that collection activity be amended accordingly, and liaison with the client must occur to allow for any necessary adjustments.

On becoming aware of a dispute, the factor's collection department will send a Notice of Dispute to the client giving full details of the query. The query will often relate to incorrect quality or quantity, discount incorrectly taken, unsatisfied specifications, or lateness in delivery. The client will be

Table 9.3   SAMPLE DEBTORS AGEING

CLIENT X.   DEBTORS AGEING AS AT 31 JANUARY 1973.

Buyer No.	Buyer Name	More than 90 days overdue	61-90 days overdue	31-60 days overdue	1-30 days overdue	Current	Total
0001	A Ltd.	245	300	42	900	1780	3267
0002	B Ltd.		55	1000	2343	875	4273
0003	C Ltd.			125	200	400	725
:	:	:	:	:	:	:	:
:	:	:	:	:	:	:	:
0026	Z Ltd.	8	90	314	604	1384	2400
	TOTAL	701	3004	4048	24390	38096	70239
		1%	4%	6%	35%	54%	100%

given a certain time, often between twenty to forty days, to clear the dispute. Normally the client is asked as to progress within the time period allowed, and if the position has not been clarified at the expiry of the agreed period, the dispute is passed back to the client, who must continue to attempt clarification in order to collect on a direct basis from the customer.

The factor attempts to assist in the clearance of disputes but does not assume any financial responsibility in this area, the client's general warranty that book debts are valid and undisputed being relevant in this situation.

LEGAL ACTION

When the factor considers it necessary to take legal action against the customer, good factor-client relationships require the factor to inform the client of this situation. In special situations, the factor may liaise with the client in a further attempt to effect collection prior to legal action. Any further stay of action at the client's request could release the factor from any obligation of assumption of bad debt loss. Even so, such a request by the client may not be agreed, as the potential recourse upon the client may be such that the factor will refuse to contemplate this course of action. This is particularly so if a heavy concentration of risks exist into the customer account under review.

9.33 Effect of the factor's collection activity

By using specialized machinery and personnel, the factor is able to adopt a professional approach in this difficult area. Standardized collection procedures, varied where necessary to achieve desired results, should reduce the delays in payments to a minimum. Moreover, the collection man should establish personal links with the purchase ledger personnel of the larger companies, allowing speedier collections from such large debtor accounts without any friction.

The techniques used by the slow payer to delay or avoid payment are met with many times, and counter-measures are developed to nullify these tactics. Identification of such customers at an early stage can avoid concentrations into slow-paying accounts and reduce the period of credit overall.

The replacement of a haphazard collection routine by the professional, systematic operation of the factor's collection department can reduce the debt turn of the smaller and medium-sized company significantly, often contributing markedly to the offset of factoring charges. Even for the large client this can still be so, and in any event the problems of routine collection activities are taken from the shoulders of senior management. A reduction in the debt turn of a client's ledger from ninety to seventy days, assuming a client borrowing cost of 10 per cent per annum, entails a saving of 0·55 per cent on sales, apart from the flexibility of a lower cash requirement to finance existing sales volume. Finally, the releasing of senior management time from mundane problems can be most noticeable, with resulting increases in efficiency in other areas of the business.

However, many factors recognize the client's ability to assist occasionally in collection, where a special relationship may exist between client and customer, or the client is willing to withhold supplies until payment has been effected. In such situations the factor, while remaining active in the collection activity, may enlist the assistance of the client.

9.4 ADDITIONAL SERVICES OFFERED

9.41 Benefits arising from contacts between senior management

Once the factoring relationship has been established, there are benefits which can arise outside the services described earlier. The extent of such benefits depends on the methods used by the factor, and the degree to which senior members of the factoring company and of the client work together.

THE ACCOUNT EXECUTIVE

All factors must develop a close relationship with the client as they become, in effect, his credit, sales accounting, and collection departments, and are closely tied to his success. A senior executive of the factor will operate as Account Executive keeping in close touch with the client, not only regarding the functioning of the factoring service, but also so as to discuss the client's general business development. Usually the Account Executive will be experienced in the problems faced by the client in his business development, and will be able to suggest the investigation of methods to increase sales, improve production efficiency, and institute financial control and planning. Knowledge of the trade can allow the Account Executive to foresee problem periods and point these out to the client.

The Account Executive projects the personality of the factoring house to the client, and to companies of importance to the client if there is any direct contact. In the long run this contact will assist in the development of additional business. Many clients find it of value to discuss their general plans and problems with a senior executive of the factoring house, who is well-versed in the problems that face their particular industry, thus assisting them to decide upon and take any necessary steps.

AREAS OF INVESTIGATION IN THE CLIENT'S BUSINESS

Moreover, the factor's personnel may visit the client regularly to ensure that procedures necessary for a proper performance of the factoring facility are being carried out. In some ways this equates to a systems audit, and the senior management of the client benefit from having various weak links pointed out, which can then be eliminated. Areas which the factor could investigate may be as follows:

(a) Are written confirmations of orders produced and sent to the customer, giving all necessary details so as to avoid later disputes?

(b) Are delivery and invoicing systems strictly controlled so that invoicing can only occur after delivery?

(c) Is evidence of delivery possible to obtain and, if so, is this effected?

(d) Is any variation of a contract confirmed by the customer's written acceptance of such variation?

(e) Is returned merchandise controlled and dealt with efficiently?

(f) If the return level is high, what is happening to quality control procedures?

(g) Are invoices raised with full information as to payment terms, delivery and order number cross references, consignment addresses, items, values, etc.?

Weakness in any of these areas can lead to disputes, loss, and inefficiency. The factor's advice is beneficial to both client and customer. In visiting the client, the factor's staff may also review financial control systems and in some cases suggest ways of investigating and establishing budgetary, cost, and cash flow controls that the management of the client may wish to implement.

ASSISTANCE OUTSIDE THE FACTORING FACILITY

Arising from the close relationship that develops, the factoring house may be able to assist in areas strictly outside the factoring facility. Many factors have banks as their shareholders and are able to promote meetings, if desired by the client, between bank and client, should the client require services offered by that bank. The client may be contemplating obtaining a loan or a public quotation, or selling part of the equity, and may well welcome an introduction to the new issue, loan, or venture capital department of the bank concerned.

The factor is able to recommend a client on the basis of past dealings, and should be well informed as to the character and capability of management besides the profitability, efficiency, and prospects of the enterprise. Alternatively, the factor may be able to recommend leasing or hire purchase facilities for his client (he may even be able to offer these facilities within his own group), and again the close relationship at senior level is of importance in this situation.

It is obvious, therefore, that a good factor can be worth more to a client than the straightforward factoring relationship implies, in the attainment of the client's ultimate objectives of growth and profitability.

9.42   Variations or developments of the factoring facility

Apart from the services which can arise from the close factor-client relationship, the factor may adapt or expand the facility itself to cater for special requirements of the client. In international trading situations he may develop 'drop shipment' arrangements or stand behind letter of credit facilities granted for the client, while domestically he may develop special credit protection procedures, enabling the client to conduct business it would otherwise have to reject.

Drop Shipment Arrangements

Drop shipment arrangements were developed by the American factors to assist the international flow of trade when American importers/distributors, the factor's clients, would obtain orders from customers. On receipt of credit approval by the factor, which would be confirmed to the overseas supplier, arrangements would be made for the supplier to ship direct to the final customer on behalf of the distributor. The factor, who would be guaranteeing payment to the supplier in respect of that specific shipment, would credit the account of the distributor upon shipment, debiting the customer. Payment made by the factor against the debt arising from the shipment would be used to pay the supplier on a direct basis for his sales value of goods so shipped. The distributor would not have physical possession of the goods, and the supplier would have the comfort of direct payment by the factor on an agreed basis.

These procedures could be modified to apply to domestic as well as to international trading, and to allow for the distributor to have physical possession of the goods. In such situations, arrangements would be confirmed so that the factor would make direct payments to the supplier, on the standing instruction of the client, upon the client (the distributor) selling identified goods of the supplier to the final customer and factoring such sales. Payments made by the factor direct to the supplier would be debited to the client's account current and would be related to the selling price of the supplier, so that the supplier received payment in relation to goods finally sold. The supplier and the distributor (the factor's client) could agree in any event a cut-off date for payment, even if goods are not sold to final customers.

This method of dealing can engender greater confidence in supplier-distributor dealings, with emphasis upon supplier credit being geared to the stock turn, and with payment by a reputable third party to the supplier on a direct basis.

SPECIAL CREDIT PROTECTION PROCEDURES

Finally, the factor may use his special expertise and market situation to review credit requests from customers of his client that, at first glance, appear to be unrealistic when related to the customer's net worth and general status. In this situation the factor may operate on the basis of factoring the customer, with a low or nil advance payment, using the factoring reserve so created to grant protection against very large credit lines on that customer, now a client of the factor. This method can be applied where the original client is, or will become, a major supplier of the customer, or if the customer is wishing to expand to a much higher level of activity.

This approach can be applied in international transactions. An actual case shows this application and the flexible approach that can be taken by the factor. In the middle of 1971, a large Dutch manufacturer and distributor of canned food products wished to sell directly to the United Kingdom by means of a distributor. The proposed distributor had good knowledge of the trade but was only just setting up as a separate trading entity upon a low capital base (less than £1,000), and as such did not justify the credit rating (£25,000 on credit terms of thirty or sixty days) necessary to facilitate and allow for development of the market for the products covered.

Contemporaneous discussions were held between the Dutch office of the Walter E. Heller International Factoring Group (N.M.B. Heller Factoring N.V) and the supplier in Holland, and H & H Factors Ltd. and the distributor in Britain. At the end of 1971, it was agreed that the parties in Holland would enter into a maturity factoring contract to cover sales to the British distributor, while the parties in Britain would enter into a factoring contract to factor sales of the distributor to the end-customers (of very good credit standing), with very low advance payments being made to cover expenses of the distributor other than the major creditor position.

H & H Factors Ltd., having investigated the creditworthiness of the final customers, having control of all debts purchased, and being satisfied with the quality of the products handled, were able to take a commercial view of the worth of the reserve due client by them. By taking a charge on that reserve, they were able to guarantee payment by their client to N.M.B. Heller Factoring N.V., who had purchased such debts from their client, the

Dutch exporter, without recourse. With satisfactory experience the credit line was increased towards the figure originally envisaged and, to assist in the build-up of stock by the client, H & H Factors Ltd. extended their credit guarantee on behalf of the client, after taking a charge on stock held by the distributor prior to sale in Britain to various customers.

From the commencement of the Factoring Agreement in Britain, H & H Factors Ltd. and the client maintained close contact, not only on matters of credit control but also in regularly reviewing client procedures and profitability. Initial expenses were more than recouped in the first full year of trading to March 1973, on sales of £140,000. By the end of 1973, the yearly sales rate of the distributor had increased to more than £300,000 and, with continuing control on expenses and overheads, profitability increased significantly so that capital employed had increased to more than £13,000. Throughout the build-up period working capital was protected against bad debts, and supplier confidence engendered as credit guarantees were extended with additional trading experience.

10 Establishing a Factoring Agreement

10.1 RECOGNIZING THE NEED FOR FACTORING

The essential point to be realized by both client and factor is that factoring cannot be used as a financial line of last resort, but only as a management tool to assist in attaining desired objectives. The client may recognize a requirement for factoring services, either in the financial or administrative field, within the context of an overall plan for future development. Budgets for future development must include use and availability of financial and management resources, and will be analyzed accordingly, so that management can see if internal, and internally generated, resources will be sufficient, and whether factoring can assist in the more productive use of such resources.

The need for factoring is therefore a derived need from the view taken by management of the future goals of the company. It is not, and cannot be, a need arising from unforeseen circumstances forcing management into hurried, or even panic-stricken, decisions in order to delay the consequences of insufficient management planning or inevitable decline. This is not to say that the factor would not give sympathetic hearing to a prospective client that had suffered a setback, but just as the banker will ask if a proposed overdraft is sufficient for the client's need, so the factor will ask what are the plans of management if the present crisis is to be overcome.

Apart from recognizing the need to increase the use of existing capital, or prevent its dilution by customer bad debts or very slow payment, the management of a company, in turning to a factor for assistance, will so do because of the need to maintain management control consequent upon a planned expansion programme.

In many cases the driving force behind the expansion of the smaller company is a manager, often also a major shareholder, whose management skills lie in the areas of either marketing or production. The need for financial planning, or overall management planning, may be taken care of, as far as the manager is concerned, by discussions once or twice yearly with auditors, while the area of credit control and regular financial control may be relegated to last place in the scale of management priorities.

With increasing sales, the imbalance of management controls often becomes apparent, as the administrative benefits of factoring are recognized by management due to force of circumstances. The factor is then asked to review a situation where a sales ledger is not under proper control. In considering a facility he then has to exercise foresight in looking beyond the present administrative problems, to the position that will arise once the sales ledger is brought under control. It is often possible to advise stricter procedures in the prospective client's offices to ensure that problems will not arise again, and the client is willing to listen readily to such advice.

Other specific applications of the factoring facility, that the prospective client may review in developing a corporate management plan, are

(a) in the area of establishing overseas subsidiaries, where the factor can send information concerning book debts factored to a central office, as well as to the actual subsidiary concerned,

(b) in granting credit protection against very large exposures on overseas or domestic distributors of the companies' products, and

(c) in assisting in management control of new companies absorbed into an existing group.

Just as the client should view the use of a factoring facility within a comprehensive plan, so the factor will want to satisfy himself that this is so, and the procedures used in establishing a factoring facility are designed to give the factor the opportunity to substantiate the reasons put forward by the client for requesting such a facility.

10.2 WHEN IS FACTORING APPROPRIATE: A CHECK LIST

Having recognized the need for factoring, the prospective client, by asking the following questions, should be able to establish whether his business is suitable for factoring: firstly that it should derive benefit from the facility, and secondly that it should possess those characteristics necessary for a number of factors to be sufficiently interested to investigate whether they should offer factoring facilities. If the questions can be answered in the affirmative, he should be able to select the appropriate factor.

(a) Are we selling to the industrial and/or commercial sector and is it desirable that we have credit guidance and protection on present and future customers?

(b) Is our average invoice value more than £75 and do we sell on average at least £1,000 per annum to each customer?

(c) Could the factor collect debts from our customers on a routine basis without our assistance? (If the prospective client is in an industry where progress payments are made, or sales are conducted on a sale or return basis, or work is subject to inspection and/or performance prior to payment, or special payment terms exist with each customer, or sales are conducted under continuing specialized contractual conditions, then the answer will be no.)

(*d*) Are our credit terms for domestic and export sales less than 180 days (preferably 90 days for domestic sales)?

(*e*) Is our sales volume more than £100,000 per annum? (If it is less, will it increase to more than this figure with the assistance of a factor?)

(*f*) Could the factor help us to expand safely into overseas markets, or establish tighter credit control in overseas or domestic subsidiaries? (These questions may not apply in every case.)

(*g*) Is our company profitable at present? Does it have a record of profitability? If it is not profitable now, will it be profitable once factoring is introduced, allowing more intensive use of working capital and management?

(*h*) Will factoring allow us to meet our budgeted plans for expansion? Are our financial resources sufficient to support such plans?

(*i*) Will we be more profitable and more efficient if we use a factor?

These questions are based upon client need and the requirements of the factor. If all questions cannot be answered affirmatively, it does not mean that the prospective client will be refused facilities by all factors he approaches. Factors do not have identical requirements. It is possible that some factors will accept clients with sales volumes below £100,000 per annum or average invoice values less than £75. However, if more than one question is answered negatively it is unlikely that the prospective client will enjoy a wide choice of factors or derive any real benefit from a factoring facility.

10.21 Industries which can benefit from factoring

Finally, it is interesting to note that certain industries can enjoy the factoring process by a process of negative selection; they are not industries where negative answers are received to the preceding questions. Capital goods industries such as heavy engineering (fabrication) or construction (roads, factories etc.) are automatically unsuitable, involving long credit terms, payments on account, progress payments or retention payments, and testing and due performance prior to payment. Those industries that remain tend to lie in the consumer durables field, such as furniture and carpets, or consumer products such as textiles, toys, shoes, and other clothing items. These are suitable for factoring.

The basic point is that factoring can be applied wherever satisfactory answers can be obtained from the preceding questions. This is true for the sale of goods and also for the rendering of services. While factoring has not made much headway in the service industries in America, the position in Europe, and elsewhere, is different. Some services are not ideally suited to the factoring process, being carried out under specialized continuing contractual conditions, but in others such as freight services, employment agencies, and plant (transport and construction equipment) hire services, factoring can be and has been applied successfully and with reasonable scope.

10.3   SELECTING THE APPROPRIATE FACTOR

10.31   Areas of inquiry

It is a mistake to assume that factoring is a homogeneous service. Factoring companies vary as to shareholders, expertise of personnel, knowledge of particular industries, method and range of conducting domestic and international business, information automatically made available, and minimum size of client. The prospective client should weigh the relative advantages and disadvantages of a number of factoring companies' facilities, prior to deciding which is the correct one for his business. In particular he should ensure that satisfactory answers to the following questions are obtained.

1. *Is the reputation of the factor and his shareholders such as to ensure that the factor will not abuse his discretionary powers?*

The powers granted to a factor under a factoring agreement are very wide-ranging and resort to these powers, for example in reducing payments against debts assigned, can be critical to the continuation of the client's business. The factor's use of such powers must always be justified by the actions of the client, and never exercised in an irresponsible manner. The main safeguard against such abuse must be the reputation of the factor and its shareholders, and the impression gained of its senior management.

2. *Is the factor able to provide an efficient service in the areas required?*

If the client is interested in obtaining full bad debt protection there is no point in approaching a factor that does not grant protection against bad debts. Assuming that the prospective client approaches two factors that operate on a without recourse basis, then the client should compare the knowledge of those factors in his particular industry, or at least obtain some guide as to the operating experience of each in his trade. Not only will this give some guide as to the ability of the factor to grant realistic credit lines, but the client can also judge whether the factor understands the peculiarities (there are often many) of the trade concerned, and would act in a commercial manner towards his customers. Finally, if a growth in exports is envisaged, how does the factor conduct international business, and what experience does he have in this field?

3. *Can the management and personnel of the factor support the aims of the factoring company?*

This question may be asked on two levels. Firstly, are the senior management likely to adopt a commercial attitude in all dealings, and do they have sufficient factoring operating experience? Secondly, are the personnel generally employed of sufficient calibre and experience to perform the necessary administrative tasks essential to the correct functioning of any factoring facility?

The client-factor situation can be much closer than any other financial or administrative relationship. Daily intercourse on matters of credit lines, clearance of disputes, collection of debts, is so large that efficient day-to-day routines must be established and supervised by the factor's management, and conducted by an efficient and experienced staff. At senior level, the staff of the factor has a far greater insight into the client's affairs and can assist in forewarning the client of difficult situations and promoting sound expansion. Senior factoring management must take a commercial, rather than a financial, view of the client's affairs and adopt positive attitudes to problems posed in the client's operations.

While this question may be difficult for the client to answer (certainly on a comparative basis), it must nevertheless be asked, as to proceed with a factor after the wrong answers have been obtained can lead to disastrous results for the client.

10.32 The question of cost

The three areas of enquiry have omitted any question of cost. This is not because cost *per se* is unimportant, since if two factors are equal in all respects then the client should choose that offering the facility at the lower rate. However, the differences that can exist between factors usually render the difference in rate immaterial. The client paying 0·1 per cent or 0·2 per cent additional fee on sales for a facility extended by a factor specializing in granting bad debt protection and collecting debts in his particular trade, or offering an efficient international service, is correct in proceeding even if the apparent cost is higher. Moreover, as the factoring industry matures so competition tends to level the rates at which facilities are offered, unless special circumstances apply.

10.4 USUAL STEPS IN ESTABLISHING A FACTORING FACILITY

10.41 The initial approach

Having recognized the need for a factoring facility, the prospective client will approach a factor, or factors, to discuss in more detail whether a factoring facility could and should be applied in his case. The approach may be made on a direct basis, following articles or advertisements seen by the prospective client, or by contact made through a supplier that is a client of the factor, or by introduction through an intermediary such as a banker, accountant, or management consultant. The first meeting is usually with the new business executive of the factor and will cover the reasons put forward by the prospective client for factoring, the exact services and benefits offered by the factoring company, and a mutual exploration as to whether both parties are likely to benefit from closer association.

10.42 Completion of the proposal form

If both sides feel investigation should be continued, the prospective client is usually requested to complete an information or proposal form which the factor will study, to reinforce the general impression gained of management and prospects. The information requested varies from factor to factor, but generally the client has to submit details covering the following points:

1. Financial situation and development of the company. It is usual for the company to submit audited accounts and internal management accounts showing the current financial situation.

2. Where a without recourse facility is being offered, the major credit exposures being, or proposed to be, undertaken. The exact names, addresses, credit outstanding, and credit terms must be detailed, so that the factor can carry out preliminary enquiries to ensure that major obstacles will not arise in this area at a later stage. Client recent bad debt experience is also often requested.

3. Workload to be assumed by the factor in administration of the sales ledger. The number and value of invoices and credit notes will be listed for the prior twelve months, or other appropriate period, as will the value of sales and credits. Additional figures of total debts outstanding and the average number of active accounts will then allow the factor to calculate the costs involved, including an allowance for bad debt write-off, on an approximate basis, so that an appropriate fee can be arrived at which can then be expressed as a percentage of sales. Apart from arriving at the fee to be quoted, the factor can also investigate any figures which give rise to

concern, such as an abnormally high returns ratio or average period of credit.

4. Further information regarding the client's affairs. Each factor will have different ideas as to what is relevant on this section. Usually, *inter alia*, the prospective client is asked to give details of shareholders, directors, auditors, bankers, and charges over the company's assets. This serves to round out the picture presented by the company.

10.43 The offer of a facility

The information built up by the factor allows an indication of the rate to be given, unless the factor believes that matters should not proceed. Confirmation of the offer of a facility, and the rates envisaged, is usually subject to a visit by senior technical personnel of the factor to the premises of the prospective client. The information given in the proposal form will be checked against supporting records, client procedures covering delivery of goods, invoicing, and acceptance of returns will be studied, and the existing sales ledger will be examined from a control and credit exposure viewpoint. Management strength and plans will be analyzed in some depth.

The company receiving confirmation of an offer should weigh the merits of each factor carefully before acceptance. Usually he should, and does, ask to visit the factor's offices to establish how the factor's procedures will fit in with his own and, of equal importance, to form a view as to whether a sound commercial relationship can be established with senior management and operating staff.

10.44 Drawing up the agreement

If both parties are satisfied that arrangements should then proceed, the factoring agreement will be drawn up and the following matters settled:

1. Are existing book debts to be factored? This decision will be based upon the client's wishes and the factor's review of the existing sales ledger. Should the client wish to sell all outstanding debts to the factor, an exhaustive survey of each customer account must be carried out. Long overdue or unreconciled accounts are usually left with the client, as are accounts the factor does not wish to handle. These often represent outstanding disputes or problems which will not be cleared by the interposition of a third party who, in any event, cannot be responsible for final settlement of technical disputes.

Any customer account transferred is usually analyzed into outstanding items of invoices and credit notes, and these are detailed to the customer in a letter (*see* 2. below), with a request that he confirm to the factor that they are outstanding. As all debts purchased by the factor may be liable to existing dispute, and as the factor may not have had an opportunity to check the creditworthiness of each customer in detail, the factor may reduce the advance against such book debts until full confirmation of debts outstanding is received from each customer.

2. The form of letters to be sent to customers explaining the introduction of the factor into the payment process. This letter should present the change in a positive light, and should be absolutely specific as to when the factor will commence to operate for the client. Factoring is a means to increased efficiency, and nothing reacts more to the detriment of this objective than a confused position for the customer, as to where payment for outstanding invoices should be sent.

3. Bankers and auditors of the client should be advised of the proposed factoring arrangements. If the bank has money extended to the client, it is advisable that the relationship of all parties be clarified.

4. A senior executive of the factoring house should be assigned to the client account to deal with all queries in the initial factoring period, and to ensure that all forms and procedures of the factor are entirely understood and acted upon by the client.

Provided that the proper groundwork has been carried out by both parties in establishing the factoring agreement, the factoring relationship should be positive, smooth, and allow for profitable expansion of the client to the benefit of both client and factor. Overlooking of problems that may arise, such as the existence of large credit exposures that the factor will not cover or of sale or return contracts which the factor will not handle, can lead to an extremely difficult relationship, which may need disentangling to the cost and embarrassment of both factor and client.

10.5 POTENTIAL DISADVANTAGES OF FACTORING

This chapter has investigated whether and how a factoring agreement should be established. In establishing an agreement, it is advisable that the pitfalls, or potential disadvantages, of factoring be appreciated. A factoring facility should be beneficial for client, customer, and factor, but this is not always so in practice. Problems can arise from a misunderstanding of the factor's role, inefficiency of the client and/or the factor, and miscalculation of the benefits arising from the factoring service.

10.51 Misunderstanding of the factor's role

The most important area of confusion between client and factor concerns disputes between client and customer. A client may tend to expect the factor to deal with all disputes until they are resolved, and may believe there is no need to retain personnel to deal with customer claims.

This expectation is entirely false. It is usual for the factor at some point to pass the disputed debt back to the client. Normally the dispute is of a technical nature and, in the final analysis, is beyond the capability of the factor who would have to revert to the client constantly if the disputed debt were not passed back to the client.

Any delay in dealing with disputes by the client will endanger the relationship with the customer. Furthermore, a client may not appreciate the necessity to pursue a disputed debt, for such debts are in fact his own sales ledger. This tardiness can cause loss to the client.

A further misunderstanding that can occur concerns the factor's ability to change a bad credit risk into a good credit risk. Further information about a customer can lead to an increase or decrease in the credit line. A client may feel that a factor is only taking credit risks that are not risks at all. This is not the case, as the factor is operating on the principle of spread of risk in reviewing customer exposures. However, in such a review danger signals emanating from individual exposures cannot be ignored.

10.52 Inefficiency of the client and/or the factor

Both the factor and the client are concerned with the expansion of the sales of the client into creditworthy customers. Each derives income from such sales. The factor has now been interposed between the client and the customer in the payment process. In many ways this could smooth the process, but inefficiency by either client or factor will have the opposite effect and may lose sales for the client.

In practice the expansion of numerous factoring clients shows this potential danger to be minimal, but individual problems can arise. If the factor sends out incorrect demands for payment or demands payment after disputes have arisen, then the customer will justifiably have cause for complaint. If the client ignores disputes, is late in sending out credit notes, or produces incorrect invoices, then problems will arise again.

The interposition of a third party in the payment process complicates such situations, and the factoring facility itself is seen as the culprit, rather than the inefficient party. This situation is analogous to a computer being blamed for producing incorrect answers from incorrect input.

10.53 Miscalculation of the benefits of factoring

A company entering into a factoring agreement does so in the belief that the benefits outweigh the cost. Benefits may arise from direct savings (sales ledger and credit control employee costs and overheads, telephone, postage, stationery, machine depreciation, credit insurance provision or premium, credit investigation cost, increased cash discount from suppliers previously foregone, a shorter period of credit extended to customers), from increased efficiency due to management concentration on production and marketing, and increased certainty of financial planning, or from increased profits from additional sales that are now possible.

To take an extreme example by way of illustration, consider a company with annual sales of £250,000, selling to twenty customers each of which is a prompt payer and is a government department, with invoice values of £1,000, which is not capable of expansion due to the small size of the market, and which has no opportunity to take cash discounts. This company is likely to be disenchanted with factoring if it had calculated that large direct savings would result from the factoring arrangement. This case could be entirely different if the customers were commercial enterprises, when such exposures could threaten continuity of the business.

It is essential for the client and the factor to examine carefully the reasons and purposes for which the factoring facility is to be used prior to entering into an arrangement, otherwise factoring may be viewed, incorrectly, as an expensive facility.

11 The Factoring Agreement

11.1 THE NATURE OF THE FACTORING AGREEMENT

The factoring agreement has to encompass the rights and obligations of the factor and client arising from the assignment or sale of the book debts of the client to the factor. It must cover the duties undertaken by the factor in return for the remuneration due to him, and should make clear the discretionary nature of the factor's rights in the financial relationship arising from his purchase of debts, and resulting payment for them to the client. In making payments for debts, often prior to collecting such debts from the final customers, the factor has to have the right to vary the timing of such payments throughout the agreement should conditions change, for example if the client insists on selling above the credit limits set by the factor.

In accepting the discretionary power of the factor, the client must be satisfied with the reputation and backing of the factor, so as to ensure that such powers will not be abused. In many ways the financial relationship depends upon mutual trust, as with a client-banker situation.

The fundamental aspects to be covered by the factoring agreement fall within four categories:

1. Legal arrangements allowing for the assignment or sale of book debts, resulting from credit sales, to the factor. The agreement will not show the factor to be taking a charge over book debts against which a loan is being made. This method of financing will reflect an invoice discounting or bank lending situation, where primary reliance would be placed upon the client's net worth and profitability, rather than upon the nature of the book debts sold to the factor.

2. Administrative functions carried out by the factor and arising from his purchase of debts. The agreement will refer to the factor's methods and liabilities in approving credit sales, the accounting relationship he enjoys with the client, and his disclosed position as a factor to the customers of the client.

3. Financial relationship arising from purchase of book debts, and the factor's discretion to reserve against disputes or difficult situations by varying the date of payment for debts purchased.

4. Duration and termination provisions.

These categories are discussed in detail in the next section.

11.2 NORMAL CONDITIONS

11.21 Conditions relating to purchase or assignment of debts

WARRANTIES BY THE CLIENT

The client, in selling or assigning debts to the factor, will make certain warranties covering the debts which must be maintained if a factoring relationship is to be sustained. The client must warrant the debts to be free from restrictions, so that the factor can purchase debts absolutely. There must not be any pledge of those debts as security to any other party, nor must any bank have a charge on such debts to secure overdraft arrangements. Moreover, not only must the debts be unencumbered but they must also be valid and enforceable at the time of purchase. The client must have supplied all the goods or rendered all necessary services represented by the invoices purchased by the factor.

There must not be any set-off or counterclaim that the customer could raise against the factor, as this would destroy the asset against which the factor makes payment. The factor attempting to collect where handles have been left off crockery, or where goods have been supplied on a sale or return basis, will lose all confidence in the affairs of the client, and if that client ceases to trade the factor may find the amounts withheld inadequate to allow for all debts that are not collectable.

FACTOR'S OBLIGATIONS

The factor's obligations under the factoring agreement are to accept the offer of debts arising from the client's credit sales. The agreement itself may even be stated to be an agreement to assign all such future debts. Debts will be accepted either at factor's risk or at client's risk according to the procedures detailed, but in any event there will usually be some mechanism whereby the factor has discretion to reject certain debts.

It is pointless for the factor to accept debts from client A due from customer C if he is suing customer C for client B, and C is unable to pay. The advice by the factor that he will not accept any further debts on customer C should be sufficient warning for client A of a perilous situation.

11.22 Conditions governing the administrative functions of the factor

CREDIT FUNCTION

The agreement must contain clauses covering the way in which credit sales under the agreement are at factor risk or at client risk, in the event that the customer is financially unable to pay. The agreement may specify that the factor must designate each credit sale into one of these classes at the time of purchase, or that such class may be automatically attributed to each invoice on the basis of the factor's prior decisions (for example, the granting of a credit line on a customer to whom the client expects to sell goods or services).

The factor is in no way responsible for disputes, and the agreement should clarify that factor risk invoices will only be written off to the factor's bad debt if the customer is unable to pay, as opposed to unwilling to pay due to a dispute concerning the goods or services supplied. In the latter situation, the factor will come off risk and only review his liability if, after the dispute is settled, the customer is shown to be unable to pay.

Once again the discretionary power of the factor is evident, as shown by his ability to withdraw a credit line on a customer should adverse knowledge of that customer come to his attention. Withdrawal can only be applied to future invoices. The client's obligation in this area is a negative one of not withholding any information which may cause the factor to withdraw credit protection on any customer.

Client risk sales are usually purchased by the factor, unless the client has been informed otherwise regarding specific customers. The client is usually stated to guarantee such sales to the factor as to their punctual payment, although the factor does not usually enforce this rule strictly, some days of grace being allowed to cater for the usual delay in settlement of debts.

ACCOUNTING FUNCTION

The agreement will recognize the accounting relationship arising from the assignment of debts by the client to the factor. Debts owing by customers of the client to the factor are not relevant in this context, except that reference is usually made to the client assisting the factor in any way necessary to facilitate the collection of such debts.

The factor purchases debts at their full face value and is immediately a debtor to the client for such amounts. Any credits issued by the client to a customer (for example for faulty merchandise returned) will reduce the value of such debts, and consequently the factor's indebtedness to the client.

Usually the agreement will state that the factor will render to the client at regular intervals, normally monthly, a statement of account showing the debts purchased by him and credited to the client, moneys paid to the client for such debts and debited to his account, and any further entries affecting the client's credit balance with the factor, such as the debiting of factoring service charges or unpaid overdue client risk invoices. There is often an obligation upon the client to agree this statement within a reasonable period of time or to lose the right to dispute the position. The due client statement sent by the factor represents the client's debtor ledger.

Payment by the factor for debts purchased can be made prior to agreed maturity or settlement dates of individual debts, or at maturity. The agreement will recognize that in making payments prior to maturity, the factor can render a charge on such payments from date of payment to maturity.

COLLECTION FUNCTION

The agreement may state explicitly that the factor has the obligation to collect debts from customers, or this may be implied by a clause stating that the client must ensure that a notation is placed on each invoice, advising the customer of the assignment of the debt and instructing that payment is to be made directly to the factor. This notification has the legal effect of requiring the customer to pay to the factor, as only the factor can give full discharge for the debt concerned. If the customer pays any other party, then it is legally possible for the factor to request further payment by the customer to the factor.

The administrative function of collection by the factor automatically follows the facts of assignment of debt, notification to the customer, and instruction to pay to the factor. While the agreement will leave collection methods at the factor's discretion, the factor will usually consult with the client before taking legal action.

Since the factor has credited the client with the value of debts purchased, and in many cases has paid for them prior to collection, it is correct and usual to find a clause in the agreement obliging the client to pay immediately to the factor any moneys received in error from customers for such debts.

11.23 Conditions governing the financial relationship of parties

Although the client is credited with the full face value of debts assigned to the factor at the time of such assignment, the method of payment by the factor can vary, and it is the method of payment contemplated by the factoring agreement that gives rise to the financial relationship between the parties.

1. The agreement can stipulate that payment will be made on a maturity date that can be ascertained by reference to the agreement. For example, the maturity date is stated to be due date plus twenty-five days allowance for slow payment. In this case the factor is guaranteeing the time of payment, and any retained reserve that is required (for example, 20 per cent of outstanding debts) should not be a constraint to this guarantee, as reserves should, in theory, be 100 per cent (with customer paying at maturity date)

and in practice should not vary to any meaningful extent below this figure. Any payment made by the factor prior to his collection of debts will not be the subject of an additional charge, as the factor is guaranteeing that only a fixed term of credit need be allowed for by the client.

2. The agreement can stipulate that the retention reserve will be 100 per cent of debtors outstanding. Again this means that the client will not receive an additional charge as the factor has no 'investment' in the client, but in this case the client is not guaranteed a fixed credit period. This clause may be used if there is insufficient trading experience to establish a maturity date.

3. The agreement may stipulate that the factor will pay up to a certain percentage, normally 80 per cent as a maximum (in the United Kingdom), of debts purchased immediately upon purchase. The balance is stated to be held as a reserve to be released upon maturity date, and subject to collection of debts outstanding. The reserve is held to support the client's obligations under the agreement, for example his guarantee to pay for overdue client risk debts, or to repay the factor where debts are disputed or credit notes issued.

An additional charge is rendered in respect of such payments by the factor, either to maturity or collection, depending upon whether a maturity date has been set. In this case, the factor has an 'investment' in the client account in that he has made payment to the client for assets (book debts) he hopes to collect.

Such payments prior to collection obviously warrant the additional charge and a very close watch by the factor on the affairs of the client, to ensure that he is meeting all his obligations under the agreement, so that collection (apart from bad debts on factor risk sales) will be effected even in the unhappy event of the client ceasing to trade.

In this situation, it is clear that the agreement must in some way give the factor discretion to vary the reserve requirement and initial payments made, should he feel justified by changed conditions. The agreement will state or imply that the reserve level can be varied unilaterally by the factor, although this right should only be exercised in a responsible manner.

For example, if there is a breakdown in the despatch administration of the client so that the factor is receiving invoices prior to delivery of goods, or in respect of goods delivered but not detailed on the invoice, then the factor may increase the reserve until he is satisfied that the problem has been cleared. Similarly, if the client concentrates sales into a few marginal customers the factor may be unhappy at the concentration of risk, both of bad debt or disputes, and may vary the reserve availability. Normally any adjustment of immediate payment or reserve requirements occurs only after consultation with the client.

The client must rely on the standing and reputation of the factor in leaving such a discretionary right with him, just as the same confidence will be given to the client's bankers, so that they will not withdraw overdraft facilities precipitously thus causing a catastrophe.

11.24   Conditions of duration and termination

The factoring relationship not only involves basic changes in the flow of working capital of the client, but also his release from many time-consuming and detailed procedures necessary for adequate control of the sales ledger. Termination of the facility is not an action which should occur at short notice, as it is often necessary for the client to set up additional specialized staff and equipment to cope with the work now contemplated. Moreover, additional working capital may be required to support sales at their present level. For these reasons it is usual for a period of notice to be written into the factoring agreement, and this is normally at least ninety days. If this is too short for the client, the factor will often extend this period.

Just as it is necessary to give a reasonable period of notice of termination, so it is of little point to enter into a factoring agreement for a short period, since it involves changes in fundamental credit control procedures for both parties. Normally a factoring agreement will run for at least one year from signing after which, in the absence of notice of termination from either party, it will continue from year to year or indefinitely, unless notice is specifically given by either party.

11.3   THE COST OF SERVICE

The factoring agreement deals with the two aspects of charges separately.

11.31   Factoring commission or service charge

A factoring commission or service charge will be detailed, normally as a percentage of the value of factored sales, and the factor's right to debit this to the client's account will be stated. This service charge will not be varied throughout the duration of the agreement except by mutual consent of the parties. This charge is based upon circumstances prevailing at the start of the facility and upon expectation of conditions that will occur during the agreement period. Should circumstances change, or prove different to expectations, then either party may attempt to vary this charge. If the other party desires to maintain the factoring agreement after the next termination date, then it may agree to a reasonable change in the charge.

Any factoring client that enters into a factoring agreement at a low service charge, consequent upon a low workload as it is selling in large individual amounts to distributors, cannot expect the factor to continue the low service charge if it changes its selling policy and starts to sell to many retail outlets, with much lower invoice values.

11.32 Additional charge

While the factoring service charge will be included without exception, the additional charge for payments will be shown only if a 'full' or 'old line' factoring facility, as opposed to a 'maturity' factoring facility, is being extended to the client. This charge is usually expressed as a charge at a real rate per annum for any payments made against invoices prior to maturity. The rate may be linked to bank base rate, finance house rate, or any other rate of easy reference, or be at the factor's discretion. In the last case, the client should expect the rate to vary throughout the agreement, in sympathy with general short-term money market rates.

12 Factoring and International Trade

The development of factoring as a commercial tool flourished under the stimulus of international trade, particularly between Britain and the United States. The benefits of factoring increased more than proportionately to the distance of the market from the client, the geographical spread of that market, and the different methods of commercial trading and languages used in the two centres of trade. If a logical case is made for employment of a factor in a domestic market situation, how much more so when the client is selling to customers abroad, wishing to pay according to their own commercial customs. The argument of economies of scale is relevant even for the largest company, and in many cases it is such a company that will be a client of the factor in the exporting field.

Factoring is often the only viable alternative to initial investment in overseas offices, and continuing administrative cost for the exporter wishing to sell abroad on open credit terms, allowing goods to be shipped to the customer and payment to be made for such goods after the normal period of credit in the country of import, and according to local custom of settlement. The alternative, which can be restrictive in allowing penetration of the market, is to operate by documentary credit within the banking system, where the importer will sign for documents of title, accepting a bill of exchange, or paying immediately to obtain such documents. Even more restrictive can be the obligation placed upon the importer to open letters of credit in the exporter's favour to allow shipments to occur.

The dispensing with letters of credit or bills of exchange by the factoring process liberalizes the import-export trading pattern, to the benefit of both parties. International trade can be conducted on an open credit basis with payments being made according to the practice of the country of the importer, without credit risk or administrative problems for the exporter. Open credit transactions across frontiers, always desirable, become practical.

12.1 METHOD OF OPERATION

The basic method of international factoring can be classified according to whether one or two factoring offices are employed.

12.11 Factor in the country of import (the import factor)

Where the client in the country of export establishes a factoring contract with the import factor, the situation is similar to the factoring arrangement in the nineteenth century between American factors and the British exporters, except for the exclusion of the marketing function then being carried out by the American factor. In general, this situation is difficult to establish, as problems of different legal systems have to be overcome, and the experience and standing of both factor and client has to be high to allow for a smooth relationship. This method is used primarily in the United States for the handling of imports and is predicated upon the unique historical experience of the American factor in this field.

In many cases, the factor will work with the selling agent of the exporter and will advance customs duties to allow clearance, possibly taking a security interest in the stock (inventory) and resulting trade debts in order to effect repayment. If the exporter is selling through an importer/distributor, the factor may establish a factoring contract with the distributor rather than the exporter, and may either guarantee credit direct to the exporter or guarantee letters of credit opened by a bank for the importer in favour of the exporter. In this case, the factor will usually take an interest in the goods, by having documents of title covering the goods shipped endorsed to his order, releasing these documents against issuance of trust receipts to the importer, and continuing the security interest in the merchandise through to the creation and assignment of the trade debts under the factoring contract. The commitment of the importer under the letter of credit is repaid out of the advances made by the factor to the client, against trade debts credited under the factoring agreement.

Guaranteeing letter of credit arrangements represents an effective financing of inventory through delivery to the importer and its warehousing, processing, and distribution period. Just as the factor will require a reserve against disputes, causing the initial payment to be less than 100 per cent of book debts purchased, so he will normally require the client (the importer) to make a cash deposit against the value of the letter of credit established, this deposit usually being 10 per cent to 30 per cent of such value. This cash deposit is to allow for any possible reduction in realizable value of the goods covered under the arrangements, and for additional payments, such as import duties, if the factor has to realize security prior to the stock being converted into book depts.

A further extension of this basis of trading is the drop shipment arrangement described in Chapter 9 (*see* page 106), where the importer/distributor does not have physical possession of the imported goods. These would be shipped direct to the customers of the distributor by the supplier, with the factor making payment to the supplier upon the security of sales proceeds guaranteed by the factor.

International trading transactions based solely upon the operations of the import factor are still general practice in America, but rarely used in other countries. This difference of approach may be attributed to the relatively greater sophistication of the American factor, coupled with a historically singular pattern of growth.

12.12   Factors in the country of import (the import factor) and export (the export factor)

As Figure 12.1 shows, four relationships are involved. Each is of interest and importance.

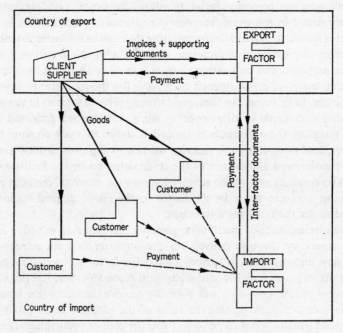

FIGURE 12.1.   Factoring relationships in international trade.

THE EXPORT FACTOR AND HIS CLIENT, THE EXPORTER/ SUPPLIER

The client will sign a factoring agreement with the export factor and assign to him export debts as they arise. Payments for debts will occur in exactly the same way as under a domestic factoring facility, and in many cases the exchange risk (if sales are conducted in the currency of the importer) can be specified and covered. For the client, apart from the requirement placed upon him to submit additional evidence to support delivery, such as copy bills of lading and insurance documentation, the factoring arrangements are identical to those governing domestic operations, the export factor being responsible for the standard functions of credit, accounting, and collection.

THE EXPORT FACTOR AND THE IMPORT FACTOR

The method by which the export factor discharges his obligations to his client will depend upon his relationship with the import factor. In many cases, the factoring offices may have common equity links and international procedures, or even a parent-subsidiary relationship. Alternatively, they may belong to a formal chain of factors agreeing upon certain rules governing the conduct of business between their offices, or may have established an *ad hoc* relationship to conduct specific transactions. In nearly every case, the import factor will have established personnel and procedures to conduct, and will be conducting, domestic factoring in the importing country.

Whatever the formal relationship, the export factor will usually 'contract out' the detailed work of credit checking, sales ledgering, and collection to the import factor for an agreed fee, possibly assigning the debts to the import factor and receiving payment on assignment, maturity, or collection. Unless business is conducted on an *ad hoc* basis, the import and export factors will work within a framework of established forms and procedures to cover decisions granted by the import factor, transmittal of documents between offices, and reporting of information such as collections.

In general, the export factor will be left to maintain an overall control of the client's export account, with the client enjoying the direct relationship with the export factor, yet obtaining the benefit arising from accounting, collection, and credit checking being undertaken by specialists in commercial procedures in the country of import.

THE IMPORT FACTOR AND THE CUSTOMER

The relationship between these two parties is established and clarified by the notation on the sales invoice documentation, stating that payment is to be made directly to the import factor. This allows the import factor to proceed as if the sale is a domestic sale, except that he will have established those additional procedures which may be necessary, such as policing the flow of documentation to allow Exchange Control procedures to be complied with, so that remittances to the import factor can be effected. The customer is often delighted to deal with an organization versed in the commercial procedures of his country. Moreover, the export factor is on hand to review and attempt to clear any disputes which may arise.

Supplier and Customer (Buyer)

In theory the relationship between the buyer and seller should be enhanced. Additional business should result from the expansion of open credit transactions, a decrease of irritation arising from collection methods understandable to the buyer and his payment to a local office, and assistance in clearing disputes. However, in practice this will not be achieved if there is any break in the efficiency of the relationships, particularly between the import factor and the export factor.

For this reason many factors, besides submitting to the disciplines of special inter-factor documentation and procedures, will establish special international departments to ensure that all documentation and correspondence is given priority, and that personnel have an understanding of international procedures as well as of domestic business. Many formal factoring groups will establish technical offices to maintain overall supervision of the conduct of international business between factoring offices.

12.2   COST

12.21   The factoring commission

The factoring commission charged to the exporter for export factoring will differ from the charge for domestic business in two ways. First, where two factoring offices are involved the charge, *prima facie*, will be higher. Secondly, against this the export factor is only involved in a general policing role, and invoice values will tend to be high in international trade. This will tend to reduce costs. The relative strength of these conflicting pressures will decide, in any individual case, whether export factoring will be more or less expensive than domestic factoring. In general, the minimum factoring commission rate can still be as low as 0·75 per cent of sales factored, but the maximum rate can approach 3·0 per cent, a rate rarely seen in domestic factoring.

12.22   Flexibility in handling export sales

The export factor will not usually insist on handling all export credit sales of a client, even though he will do so for domestic business. Many permutations can be found, where all or no domestic business is being factored and some or all foreign markets are being handled by the factor. The whole turnover requirement is usually upheld within each export market although, for very large clients, this may be further restricted as to particular operating divisions. The minimum sales per annum figure of £100,000 is not generally adhered to, especially for the large domestic client wishing to develop export markets from a very low base. Should payments be required from the factor prior to maturity, the same additional charge as in domestic business is usually rendered to the client.

12.23 Cost effectiveness

In many ways, the cost effectiveness of export factoring can be measured more accurately than for domestic business. An exporter expecting sales of £100,000 in a new market abroad, and having decided that to achieve this he should sell through an agent on the same credit terms to customers in that market as the indigenous manufacturer, can compare a factoring charge of, say, £2,000 for the year against the cost of operating an office to effect credit investigation and credit protection, detailed ledgering and local collection. The overheads of office rental and specialized personnel make any such comparison, at least up to sales figures of £500,000 per annum, a very favourable one for the factoring house. The exporter cannot spread his fixed costs over more than the individual market, while the factor is spreading such costs over many domestic and export factoring clients.

Table 4.1 (*see* page 37) is applicable to export factoring, as an extreme case of the argument for spreading indivisible resources over a sufficient workload. This argument is realized not only for the medium-sized company wishing to export for the first time, and for whom factoring may be the only practical vehicle into the export field, but also for the very large corporation wishing to branch out into additional export markets or to develop existing markets in more depth. For the latter company, the degree of efficiency desired in overseas credit control, to match domestic requirements, can be achieved at very low comparative costs.

12.3 THE SCOPE OF INTERNATIONAL FACTORING

International factoring generally depends upon an import factor having a strong domestic operation, and thus having generated the skills necessary to service, on a detailed basis, the requests of the export factor emanating from the exporter's sales. In this context, it is interesting to note that while the American-British trade in the nineteenth century saw the birth of factoring as it is known today, factoring has nevertheless established strongholds

Table 12.1   INTERNATIONAL SCOPE OF FACTORING

Country	Year Factoring Established	Number of Factoring Houses	Factoring Volume 1973 (millions)	Comments on Operations
Australia	1959	5	A $130	Primarily with recourse factoring. Imports usually handled by confirming houses. Banking influence strong.
Belgium	1963	5	B Fr 5,000	Primarily without recourse factoring. Much international business via Walter E. Heller, International Factors, Credit Factoring International groups, and Factors Chain International. Major banks and credit insurance companies are involved in factoring companies.
Canada	1930/1935, but real growth since 1960	6	$500	Primarily without recourse factoring, in yarn and textile industries only. American bank influence strong and Canadian bank influence increasing.
Denmark	1965	4	D Kr 0·6	Primarily with recourse factoring, except for international transactions.
France	1964	5	F Fr 1,500	Primarily without recourse factoring. International factoring probably less than 10% of total volume.
West Germany	1958	20	DM 2,000	Primarily with recourse factoring. Of all factoring houses, approximately six can be expected to grow into major operations.
Hong Kong	1972	2	US $10	Mainly export factoring at present.
Italy	1964	4	Lr 90,000	Primarily with recourse factoring. Banking influence is strong and likely to increase.
Netherlands	1965	4	Hfl 500	Primarily without recourse factoring. Banking influence is strong.
Norway	1961	15	N Kr 2,000	Primarily with recourse factoring, but without recourse factoring increasing in importance. All major banks and insurance companies are involved in factoring.

Country				Description
Portugal	1966	2	$600	Very small amount of international transactions.
South Africa	1957	15	Rd 200	Five factors constitute major part of the industry. Primarily with recourse factoring.
Spain	1965	4	Pes 3,500	Primarily without recourse factoring. Banking influence is strong.
Sweden	1965	6	S Kr 5,200	All factoring companies are associated with banks, are part of international factoring networks, and do not take the bad debt risk.
U.K.	1960	9	£250	Primarily without recourse factoring, but a few important exceptions in the factoring industry. Bank influence very strong and increasing. International factoring expected to grow, together with domestic volume.
U.S.A.	Present form dates from late nineteenth century	at least 30 major factors	$16,000	Longest established factoring market, and the largest. Credit risk bearing seen as essential to the factoring function. Still very tied to the textile and allied industries (more than 70% of volume). Very low volume of international business, mainly servicing imports. Bank influence growing very rapidly (share of volume by bank factors increased from 33·8% in 1970 to 49·7% in 1972).

Notes:

1. Number of factoring houses given relates to established factoring houses or those with substantial shareholders just starting factoring operations. Figure is given as a guide and, where necessary, qualified in last column.

2. Figures for U.S.A. relate to those given by National Commercial Finance Conference Inc., whose membership covers up to 90 per cent of U.S.A. factoring industry.

3. Details given in columns 2, 3, and 4 are estimates only, intended to give a broad picture of the local factoring situation.

Source: Associated offices of Walter E. Heller Overseas Corporation.

throughout many world markets. This has been due either to a deliberate geographical expansion of an individual factoring group to service the export needs of its existing or potential clients, or to the setting up of indigenous factoring companies by financial institutions in those markets, to service an expected need.

12.31   World involvement

Table 12.1 shows this involvement in the countries listed, and in many cases the strength of the supporting institutions demonstrates that expansion of factoring in such markets, either on a domestic or international basis, has far to travel if it is to justify the interests and investments involved.

Table 12.1 also shows that whereas, in general, the distinguishing characteristic of factoring as practised in Britain and America is the purchase of debts without recourse to the client in the event of customer inability to pay, there are at least six countries where this is not the case. It is too early to say whether this difference will disappear as companies develop the expertise and desire to grant protection against bad debts, prompted by a demand for this aspect of the service.

Another important aspect shown by the table is that even though factoring is not regarded as a lending operation, it is subject to increasing influence throughout the world by banking institutions, who view factoring as a method of expanding the financial services offered to their customers.

Finally, by relating the information about the number of factoring companies in each country to the international markets served by the Credit Factoring International, International Factors, Factors Chain International and Walter E. Heller factoring groups, through their associates or subsidiaries, one can see the prime importance of these groups in many countries throughout the world. Today it is clear that international factoring can be conducted in many major markets, on the basis of an established domestic factoring industry. The position in the United Kingdom contains many interesting features in considering the potential development of international factoring.

12.32   Role of the United Kingdom

The United Kingdom has played an important role in the development of the factoring process. The factoring industry now has a strong domestic base, in terms of institutional support, which should lead to further growth. A country where international transactions account for approximately 25 per cent of gross national product should be receptive to a commercial tool allowing for an expansion of open credit transactions across international frontiers, particularly with participation in an enlarged European Common Market. Against this background it is interesting to note from Table 3.2 (*see* page 24) the involvement of the major factoring houses in international factoring operations.

Table 12.2 sets out in more detail the context within which each United Kingdom factoring house conducts international factoring. The basic division lies between those factors that are part of a loose or closely-knit international group, and those subscribing to Factors Chain International, a chain of independent factors operating international factoring according to agreed common procedural rules. As opposed to the three groups encompassing Credit Factoring International Ltd., H & H Factors Ltd., and International Factors Ltd., the Factors Chain International is an open chain allowing any number of factors from one country to participate. In Great Britain, Alex Lawrie Factors Ltd., Arbuthnot Factors Ltd., and Griffin Factors Ltd., are all members.

Many of the groups reflect the growing recognition of the factors that successful international factoring procedures entail a high degree of operating efficiency and liaison between offices. For example, the Factors Chain International has a four-man secretariat in Amsterdam to assist in standardizing procedures between participating offices, while the Walter E. Heller group, encompassing H & H Factors Ltd., has set up a technical office in Utrecht to assist in increasing operating efficiency between European offices.

The increasing importance of international factoring to the British factoring industry is demonstrated from the few figures that are available. H & H Factors Ltd. reported in early 1973 that the amount of international business handled as a percentage of total portfolio increased from under ten per cent at the end of 1971 to approximately twenty per cent by the end of 1972, with further increases expected in 1973. In April 1973 it was reported that the international business of International Factors Ltd. was running at approximately twenty-two per cent of total business. Growth in this area should continue when these figures are compared with the general average of forty per cent reported from the Walter E. Heller European offices in 1972, excluding H & H Factors.

Table 12.2   MAJOR U.K. FACTORS—FORMAL LINKS FOR CONDUCTING INTERNATIONAL FACTORING TRANSACTIONS

Factor	International Group	Ownership Links	Technical Liaison and Control	Markets covered by Group
Alex Lawrie Factors Ltd.	Factors Chain International	None	General co-ordinating Secretariat. Headquarters in Amsterdam.	Austria, Belgium, Canada, Denmark, Finland, France, Israel, Italy, Netherlands, Norway, South Africa, Spain, Sweden, Switzerland, U.K., U.S.A., West Germany.
Arbuthnot Factors Ltd.	Factors Chain International	None	General co-ordinating Secretariat. Headquarters in Amsterdam.	Austria, Belgium, Canada, Denmark, Finland, France, Israel, Italy, Netherlands, Norway, South Africa, Spain, Sweden, Switzerland, U.K., U.S.A., West Germany.
BankAmerica — WilliamsGlyn Factors Ltd.	Bank of America (banking offices)	Bank of America	No special office for this function.	Throughout world where banking offices maintained.
Barclays Factoring (Part of Barclays Export & Finance Co. Ltd.)	Full international factoring services not yet provided.			
Credit Factoring International Ltd.	Own network of overseas offices	U.K. company owns offices overseas	U.K. company controls overseas office by use of Multi-national Computer Centre in U.K. Overseas offices responsible for local client and customer relationships.	Austria, Belgium, Canada, Denmark, Finland, France, Ireland, Italy, Netherlands, Norway, Sweden, Switzerland U.K., U.S.A., West Germany

Company	Network	Ownership	Organisation	Countries
Griffin Factors Ltd.	Factors Chain International	None	General co-ordinating Secretariat. Headquarters in Amsterdam.	Austria, Belgium, Canada, Denmark, Finland, France, Israel, Italy, Netherlands, Norway, South Africa, Spain, Sweden, Switzerland, U.K., U.S.A., West Germany.
H & H Factors Ltd.	Walter E. Heller International	Walter E. Heller Overseas Corporation holds majority or substantial minority interest in all companies. Balance usually held by local banks or finance institutions.	Central office in Utrecht for co-ordination of European administration. Overseas office in Chicago for total world-wide co-ordination.	Argentina, Australia, Belgium, Canada, Denmark, France, West Germany, Hong Kong, Israel, Italy, Mexico, Netherlands, Norway, Philippines, Portugal, Singapore, South Africa, Spain, Sweden, U.K., U.S.A.
International Factors Ltd.	Associate Offices	Majority holding by local banks.	Group controlled by Annual Chairman's Meeting (strategy) and the President and Officers of the Managers (tactical).	Australia, Austria, Belgium, Canada, Denmark, Finland, France, West Germany, Israel, Italy, Japan, Netherlands, New Zealand, Norway, Portugal, South Africa, Spain, Sweden, Switzerland, U.K., U.S.A.
Factoring Division of Mercantile Credit Co. Ltd.	None	None	Administration for export sales handled from U.K. Reciprocal collection arrangements with European Finance Companies.	U.K. and Europe

Source: Individual factors listed.

Index